THE SALVATION ARMY
HANDBOOK OF DOCTRINE

THE SALVATION ARMY

Handbook
of
Doctrine

INTERNATIONAL HEADQUARTERS

GENERAL ORDER

This volume contains an exposition of the principal Doctrines of The Salvation Army as set forth in its Deed Poll of 1878.

These Doctrines are to be taught in connection with all Salvation Army officers' training operations, both preparatory and institutional.

It is required of officers of all ranks that their teaching, in public and private, shall conform to these eleven Articles of Faith.

INTERNATIONAL HEADQUARTERS,
LONDON, E.C.4.

MADE AND PRINTED IN GREAT BRITAIN
IN UNIVERS AND BASKERVILLE TYPE
BY THE CAMPFIELD PRESS, ST. ALBANS, HERTS.

CONTENTS

THE DOCTRINES OF
THE SALVATION ARMY

(As set forth in the Deed Poll of 1878)

1. We believe that the Scriptures of the Old and New Testaments were given by inspiration of God; and that they only constitute the divine rule of Christian faith and practice.

2. We believe there is only one God, who is infinitely perfect—the Creator, Preserver and Governor of all things—and who is the only proper object of religious worship.

3. We believe that there are three persons in the Godhead—the Father, the Son and the Holy Ghost—undivided in essence and co-equal in power and glory.

4. We believe that in the person of Jesus Christ the divine and human natures are united; so that He is truly and properly God, and truly and properly man.

5. We believe that our first parents were created in a state of innocency but, by their disobedience, they lost their purity and happiness; and that in consequence of their fall all men have become sinners, totally depraved, and as such are justly exposed to the wrath of God.

6. We believe that the Lord Jesus Christ has, by His suffering and death, made an atonement for the whole world, so that whosoever will may be saved.

7. We believe that repentance toward God, faith in our Lord Jesus Christ, and regeneration by the Holy Spirit are necessary to salvation.

8. We believe that we are justified by grace, through faith in our Lord Jesus Christ; and that he that believeth hath the witness in himself.

9. We believe that continuance in a state of salvation depends upon continued obedient faith in Christ.

10. We believe that it is the privilege of all believers to be 'wholly sanctified', and that their 'whole spirit and soul and body' may 'be preserved blameless unto the coming of our Lord Jesus Christ' (1 Thess. 5: 23).

11. We believe in the immortality of the soul; in the resurrection of the body; in the general judgment at the end of the world; in the eternal happiness of the righteous; and in the endless punishment of the wicked.

1

THE STUDY OF DOCTRINE

Section I. INTRODUCTION

The word 'doctrine' means 'teaching', as can be seen from Matt. 7: 28: 'The people were astonished at His doctrine', and Mark 4: 2: 'And He . . . said unto them in His doctrine . . .'. This is true of the other forty-nine occasions where the word appears in the Authorized Version of the New Testament. The same word is also used to describe teaching of a varied and conflicting nature, for example, 'the apostles' doctrine' (Acts 2: 42), 'the doctrine of the Pharisees and of the Sadducees' (Matt. 16: 12), 'divers and strange doctrines' (Heb. 13: 9). *

1. The doctrine studied in this Handbook is:

(a) *theological*, because it deals with the nature and purpose of God;

(b) *ethical*, because its teaching is related to human conduct;

(c) *Christian*, because it is based upon the revelation of God in Christ as set forth in the Scriptures. This completes and interprets all other knowledge of God given to men.

2. Christian doctrine is:

(a) *indispensable*, for it provides guide-lines for the right use of all other knowledge;

(b) *fundamental*, for by it alone can man know the reason for his existence and the direction his life should take;

(c) *essential*, for it deals with truths which ultimately will be

* Where no other indication is given references are to the Authorized (King James) Version.

I

the only facts that matter. Here is given the reason for man's separation from God with its consequent distress, but here is also to be found the way in which this broken fellowship can be restored.

3. The study of doctrine—indeed, the subject itself—has certain limitations:

(a) *We cannot go beyond what God Himself has been pleased to disclose.* No one has authority to exceed God's own revelation of His saving will.

The truths revealed by God are given to make us ' wise unto salvation '. This is their very practical end. They are not intended to provide material for indefinite speculation. When Jesus Himself was asked questions which were merely speculative, His answer was to turn the inquirer's attention to the salvation of himself and his fellows (Luke 13: 23, 24; John 21: 20–22; Acts 1: 6–8).

(b) *Finite man is not capable of fully understanding infinite revelation even should this be given.* Man cannot comprehend in all its fulness the mystery of divine truth. He knows in part and he prophesies in part (1 Cor. 13: 9).

(c) *Divine truth has to be stated within the limitations of human language.* Illustrations and analogies can become strained beyond their limits in our endeavour to present timeless truths. This means that some words are given a value beyond their normal usage. Where this is so, we should keep such words in their scriptural context, making it clear—for instance—that when we speak of love we mean the holy and redeeming love of God.

(d) *The study of doctrine has also to recognize man's spiritual condition.* The man who says that he can see nothing in the Bible is not judging the Bible but himself (1 Cor. 2: 14, N.E.B.). Both Old and New Testaments refer to man's ' deadness ', ' blindness ' and ' hardness of heart ' where revelation is concerned. Nowhere is this more apparent than in the reaction of men to Jesus, the light of the world (John 1: 5, 10, 11, N.E.B. See also John 8: 43; Acts 13: 27).

Man needs sight as well as light; spiritual truths are spiritually discerned. To the natural man the things of God are foolishness. It is as we do God's will that we prove the truth of the doctrine (John 7: 17. See also Matt. 6: 22, 23; John 14: 17; 2 Cor. 4: 4, 6).

4. Nevertheless, the revelation of God in Christ provides an adequate answer to the three difficulties outlined above.

(*a*) *Jesus gives a revelation that is adequate (John 1: 18), one that ' sufficeth us '.*

(*b*) *He is the revelation of God in terms of a human life.*

(*c*) *His atonement can deal with the root cause of man's spiritual blindness—his sin.*

5. Any introduction to a Handbook of Doctrine must make it clear that the Salvation Army Articles of Faith follow the main outline of historic Christian teaching as derived from the Scriptures.

As Catherine Booth said in 1883 when dealing with the Army's relationship to the churches:

> Neither are we diverse from the Churches in the great fundamental doctrines of Christianity. We have not adopted any of the new gospels of these times. We have not given up any of the fundamental doctrines of Christianity, such as the fall, the universal call to repentance, justification by faith through Jesus Christ, a life of obedience, heaven and hell (*The Salvation Army in Relation to the Church and State*, p. 30).

At the beginning the Founder was against any thought of forming a new sect or encouraging further division in the Church.

' This is an unsectarian mission,' he wrote in September, 1867, in the first annual report of The Christian Mission. ' Our creed is the Bible, our work is to publish the gospel, and we welcome as co-workers all who hold the word of God as the standard of faith and practice and whose hearts are in sympathy with revival work.'

3

Thus the Statement of Doctrine which he prepared was designed to provide a basis of scriptural essentials which his first helpers—a number of whom already belonged to an existing section of the Church—could accept without contradiction of what they already believed. This simple statement was therefore:

(a) *evangelical*—emphasizing the teaching necessary to bring sinners to a knowledge of God's saving grace, and believers to the experience of holiness;

(b) *spiritual*—as opposed to ceremonial, emphasizing that the Spirit of God could communicate with the spirit of man without any set ritual or material means. The only mediator between God and man is Jesus Christ, the righteous. Every soul who looks to God in repentance and faith will receive the blessing of salvation (see chap. 8) independent of time or place.

Certain aspects of theology are not mentioned in the Army's Articles of Faith—for the very good reason that this statement was designed to serve our evangelical mission. For example, nothing is said of the duty of believers to work for the salvation of others. The explanation is that those for whom this statement of faith was first drawn up were themselves already practising evangelists. The converts won by them were soon instructed that they too were saved to save.

This point was covered by linking to the affirmation of faith a pledge (*The History of The Salvation Army*, Vol. 1, Appendix G.), one item of which read:

> We agree to set our hearts upon the salvation of souls, and to put forth constant personal effort to secure the salvation of sinners.

With minor alterations in phrasing this principle is preserved in the present Articles of War (para. 8).

6. To sum up, the practical implications of Salvation Army teaching are that:

(a) *All men are sinners in need of salvation.*

(b) *The atonement made by Jesus avails for all.*

(*c*) *Conversion is an inward spiritual change wrought by the Holy Spirit.*

(*d*) *Salvation from sin should lead to holiness of life.*

The place of doctrine in the life of the Army is central. Our very title draws attention to our doctrine and mission, and the flag, crest and motto all share this same significance.

Section II. A BRIEF SURVEY OF SALVATION ARMY DOCTRINE

1. No Article of Faith stands by itself. All aspects of doctrine need to be considered in relation to one another.

To fail to do this with any Article of Faith is to do injustice to all. Salvation Army doctrine is not a collection of isolated facts but a related unity which is both theological—that is, having to do with God—and evangelical—having to do with man's salvation.

To summarize:

Article 1 makes clear that the Bible is our authority for both teaching and practice.

Articles 2 *and* 3 declare that there is one God, Father, Son and Holy Spirit, the Creator, Preserver and Governor of the universe which is His handiwork.

Article 4 sets out the doctrine of the Incarnation.

Article 5 deals with man's sinfulness and his consequent need of restoration.

Article 6 has to do with the nature and efficacy of the Atonement.

Articles 7 *to* 10 deal with the work of grace in the lives of those who accept salvation.

Article 11 sets the whole of these truths against the background of eternity.

2. In addition, these articles declare God to be:

(*a*) *Creator, Preserver and Governor*—Article 2.

(*b*) *Redeemer*—Articles 4 and 6–10.

(*c*) *Revealer of the truths set out in the Scriptures*—Article 1.

All the teaching given in the articles must be combined. It is the one God who is Creator, Preserver, Governor, Redeemer and Revealer. He fulfils His purpose in all His works; He governs in all realms; He will bring all things to their final consummation (Article 11).

The supreme object of divine activity is the salvation of man (Articles 1, 2, 4, 6–10).

The revelation of God's saving purpose was committed first to the people of Israel, and then to the new Israel—the Church of God, of which The Salvation Army is an integral part. Thus man himself has become an agent in God's saving work, and the Army's divine commission is to make Jesus known as Saviour.

2. The Army's message can thus be summarized:

(*a*) *Man's fellowship with God has been broken by his own sinfulness and he cannot restore this by his own efforts* (Article 5).

(*b*) *God has acted to remedy this situation* (Articles 4 and 6).

(*c*) *Man's response in penitence and faith will result in his salvation* (Articles 7–10).

Further truths are given in Articles 2 and 3 about the God who saves, and the bearing of conduct in this life upon the life which is to come is dealt with in Article 11.

2

THE BIBLE AS THE BASIS OF CHRISTIAN DOCTRINE

' We believe that the Scriptures of the Old and New Testaments were given by inspiration of God; and that they only constitute the divine rule of Christian faith and practice ' (Article 1).

Section I. INTRODUCTION

This statement is the first of the eleven Articles of Salvation Army belief because the Bible is the source from which all our doctrine is derived, and the authority to which appeal is made in all doctrinal inquiry.

The basic claim is that God Himself is the authority behind our teaching—here referred to as ' the divine rule ', while the Bible is presented as being the means God has used to reveal those truths which are of saving importance to man.

Part of the earliest Salvation Army statement (appearing in the Army's first Doctrine Book, 1881) concerning the purpose of the Bible reads:

> God has caused His mind on the subject of our deliverance, duty and destiny to be written and preserved in this volume, so that this book really contains the statement of His judgment and will concerning mankind, and is, therefore, the word of God, or the revelation of His mind on the subject.

This particular Article of Faith covers the following points:

(*a*) *The Scriptures of the Old and New Testaments are the means God has used to give us the truths we hold as doctrine.*

(*b*) *These writings are unique in that ' they only ' have this qualification.*

(c) The words ' given by inspiration of God ' define their relationship to all other writings and describe the manner by which these truths have been given.

Section II. THE AUTHORITY OF THE SCRIPTURES

The Bible (the Scriptures of the Old and New Testaments) is the book upon which The Salvation Army bases both its faith (its doctrine) and its practice (its pattern of Christian living).

The word *Bible* is derived from a Greek word meaning *book*. By calling it *the* Bible we mean that it is *the* book or the Book of books. By calling it *Holy* we mean that it is given of God. It is both a book and a collection of books, and is therefore described as a divine library.

The Bible is also called ' Scripture ' (meaning ' writing '), ' The Scriptures ' and ' The Holy Scriptures ', because it is the written record of God's message to mankind.

1. The nature of biblical authority.

The authority of the Bible (the Scriptures) rests entirely upon the validity of its claim to be the divinely inspired record of God's disclosure of Himself and His saving purpose for mankind.

The subjects with which the Bible deals are the most important that can occupy the mind of man and are those which present him with his deepest problems. The Bible tells him of God, his Maker and the Author of all things, and of God's will concerning man. It reveals to him the way of deliverance from sin, and the source of power to live a godly life through Christ. It informs him about the world to come and indicates the final destinies of the saved and the unsaved.

The study of Christian doctrine begins with the assumption of the authority of the Bible. This assumption is justified by the testimony of the Christian Church through twenty centuries, and is validated by the experience of countless believers of many races who have proved the truth of its teaching in their lives. Section IV below describes why the Bible can be accepted as an authentic record of the truths of the Christian Faith. For the inquiring believer there will be the added witness of the Holy Spirit, who will quicken his mind and soul so that he may perceive and understand the truth within its pages.

The authority of the Bible, then, is that of the written record of the redemptive activity of God through which man encounters God and learns of His will and purposes. In this connection the Bible is:

(a) Unique

Man can reason and can discover many truths about himself and the universe in which he lives. He can even express theories regarding the possibility of the existence and nature of a divine Being. But without the divine self-disclosure which is recorded in the Scriptures man would not arrive at the conclusion that ' God was in Christ reconciling the world to Himself ' (2 Cor. 5: 19).

William Booth declared the Bible to be ' the only authorized and trustworthy written revelation of the mind of God. In this, it stands alone, not one among other such scriptures ' (*The Bible, its Divine Revelation, Inspiration and Authority*, p. 24).

(b) All sufficient

The Salvationist recognizes no other writing or authority to be equal to the Bible in the realm of Christian faith and practice. His doctrinal position and his standard of Christian living find their warrant in the Bible. As he does not accept dogma which lacks scriptural authentication he may not observe all the traditional practices of the historic churches, but in the essential truths of the Faith he is in fundamental agreement with his Christian brethren.

William Booth wrote that the Bible ' gives us everything in the way of a written revelation that is necessary to salvation, holy living and our welfare '. Such, too, is the verdict of:

Athanasius, Bishop of Alexandria (fourth century A.D.)

The holy and divinely inspired Scriptures are of themselves sufficient to the enunciation of truth (*Contra Gentes*, i).

9

Augustine of Hippo (fifth century A.D.)

In those things which are plainly laid down in Scripture, all things are found which embrace faith and morals (*On Christian Doctrine*, ii).

2. The Scriptures and other authorities.

The Salvation Army's Articles of Faith are in accord with the truths contained in the ancient Christian creeds known as the Apostles' Creed and the Nicene Creed. These creeds are not, however, substitutes for the Scriptures, for their authority is derived from them. Yet they have an important complementary value in their statement and interpretation of the essential truths of the Christian Faith.

In any exposition of the Christian Faith The Salvation Army takes into account the traditional interpretations of the Christian Church, believing that no Scripture is of purely private interpretation. We do not, however, give an unqualified acceptance to what is generally termed the traditions of the Church, for while we respect them and those who follow them, we do not hold ourselves bound by any practices or teachings not possessing valid scriptural authority.

In considering these *secondary* authorities, a place is found for reason. Though the Christian religion calls for faith it cannot be described as contrary to reason. The place of reason in relation to revelation is shown in sect. III.

3. The meaning of faith in relation to doctrine.

The word *faith* as used in this connection means more than the *act of believing*. It embraces *the doctrines or beliefs held and taught*. It is ' the Faith ', to which reference is made in 1 Tim. 4: 1; 6: 21; 2 Tim. 1: 13 (' an outline of the sound teaching ', N.E.B.).

Doctrines are concise statements of those biblical truths which are vital to Christian experience. Doctrines, however, as articles of belief, may be held in the mind without having any positive effect upon life and conduct. It is therefore essential that the Christian makes a full commitment to God on the basis of his personal faith in these truths.

When this is done two things happen. The Holy Spirit, who inspired those through whom the Scriptures were given, will, by His indwelling presence, provide the believer with the inward witness both to the authority of the Scriptures and to the validity of the doctrines derived therefrom. He will also, by His transforming work in the life of the believer, translate these great truths of the Faith into that authentic expression of Christian living which we call the spirit of Salvationism.

4. Archaeology and the Bible.

While archaeology can often be found to corroborate the historical statement of the Bible, it cannot *prove* or *disprove* the essential truths that constitute ' divine revelation '. Truth lies deeper than historical records. We accept the Christian Faith because we are persuaded that it is the truth about God, because we see in Jesus the answer to the problem of sin and of evil, and because we believe there is salvation for all.

From many examples of archaeological corroboration of biblical records, the following can be cited:

(*a*) The Bible account of an invasion of Palestine in the time of Abraham (see Gen. 14) has been confirmed by the discovery of an inscription on an ancient ruin of the names of all four invading kings.

(*b*) Outside the Bible no ancient writer was known who mentioned the Hittites, but inscriptions discovered in Turkey show that the Hittites were once a leading nation in Western Asia, almost as important as the Assyrians or the Egyptians.

(*c*) The discovery of the Dead Sea Scrolls includes manuscripts—dating around the time of Christ—of some Old Testament writings (for example, parts of Isaiah); that is, they are over one thousand years older than the Masoretic text from which the Authorised Version of 1611 was translated.

(*d*) The accuracy of Luke as an historian has also been confirmed. For instance, he is precise in calling magistrates of the cities of Asia Minor and Greece by their right titles. Again, inscriptions confirm what had once been doubted, that Jupiter and Mercury were worshipped in the vicinity of Lystra.

These and similar discoveries do not, taken alone, prove the authority and inspiration of the Bible, but they support its trustworthiness in many matters of historical fact, and help to confirm our confidence in its reliability in other respects.

Section III.   THE MEANING AND NATURE OF REVELATION

' Revelation ' is the ' unveiling ' or the making known of what otherwise would remain hidden.

1.   Divine revelation

is the making known by God of the truth concerning Himself and His will for mankind. This is of two kinds:

(*a*) *General or natural revelation* is that knowledge of God and divine truth which may be obtained by reflecting on:

> (i) The work of God *around us*. Much in nature testifies to the wisdom and power of God.

> (ii) The work of God *within us*. Our sense of dependence and our conscience suggest Someone on whom we can depend and a Lawgiver to whom we are accountable.

> (iii) The work of God *in history*. There is evidence in history to show that those who disregard the laws of God bring the consequences of their disobedience on their own heads (Gal. 6: 7).

(*b*) *Special or supernatural revelation* is that knowledge of divine truth which is given directly by God to man, and which man could not have discovered by general revelation alone. The Bible is the record of this revelation.

2. Natural revelation

is available to all and man is responsible to use the measure of light bestowed upon him. Thus the Bible shows that man can receive revelation of God through *nature* (Ps. 19: 1, 2; Rom. 1: 19, 20, N.E.B.), *conscience* (Acts 17: 23) and *history* (Isa. 14: 4–6; Prov. 14: 34; Ezra 1: 1).

3. Natural revelation alone is insufficient

seeing that:

(*a*) *It provides but limited knowledge of God.* For example, it says little of His holiness and love, or of His purposes for man's future.

(*b*) *It sheds no light on man's greatest need*—a way of deliverance from sin.

(*c*) *It has failed* to lead any race or people to the knowledge of God given in the Bible.

4. Man needs the supernatural revelation

recorded in the Bible, otherwise he could know nothing of God's redemptive action through Jesus Christ. The Bible reveals to man his fallen state, and declares that because man cannot rise to God, God has come to man. Further, that as parents suffer if their children are lost, so God, the Heavenly Father, suffers over His lost and erring children. Without supernatural revelation man could not have perceived these truths.

5. God's special or supernatural revelation to man was given through chosen and prepared agents and in different ways (Heb. 1: 1, 2, N.E.B.).

In early times Abraham and his descendants (the people of Israel) were chosen to receive, guard and record divine truth on behalf of mankind. For this purpose they were set apart as a ' peculiar people ', that is, God's very own. God spoke to them through their rise and fall as a people so that their faith came to be expressed in a recital of the acts of God (Ps. 106).

God's supreme and culminating revelation came, however, in His Son, Jesus Christ, whose words and works are recorded in the Gospels. It is the fulness of the revelation in Christ which makes apparent the fragmentary nature of the revelation of ' former times '.

6. The divine revelation contained in the Bible was gradually completed.

For instance, there is evidence of a growing and deepening understanding of:

(a) *The nature of God.* Through their history, and especially through their prophets, the Jewish people came to a deeper understanding of the true nature of God. This revelation reached its climax in Jesus Christ who fully made known God's fatherhood and holy love (Heb. 1: 2, 3).

(b) *The standard for man's conduct.* In the law and in the prophetic writings there is evidence of a gradual ennobling of the moral standards of the Jewish people. The highest development, however, is to be found in the teaching of Jesus, who stressed the inward, spiritual nature of ' the law written in the heart '. This can be seen in Mark 12: 28–33, where love to God and man is described as the fulfilment of the Law, and in Matt. 5: 21–48, where external conformity is shown to be validated only by inward obedience.

(c) *God's plan of salvation.* God's promise to redeem His people was variously interpreted throughout Old Testament times, often in terms of a rather narrow nationalism. Its true spiritual nature was increasingly perceived by certain of the prophets, who glimpsed the truth which found its fulfilment in Jesus Christ (see Luke 24: 25–27, N.E.B.).

(d) *The future life.* In Old Testament times the revelation given was comparatively scanty, but through Jesus was made known the promise of eternal life. (Compare Isa. 26: 19 and Dan. 12: 2 with Luke 20: 37, 38; John 11: 23–26. See also chap. 11 of the Handbook.)

7. Jesus Christ is God's supreme revelation to man.

To those who deny supernatural revelation, Jesus Christ is someone beyond their understanding. Sometimes He is represented as the best and noblest of men, a martyr to His convictions, but no more. According to this view, however, He must have been either self-deceived or an impostor, both suppositions being quite inconsistent with what is recorded of Him. Should the assertion be made that in fact Christ never lived, then some explanation needs to be given as to how there arose so remarkable an assessment of his life, death and rising again as is given in the New Testament.

Concerning the supreme revelation of God in Christ:

(a) *The most striking feature* was His perfect oneness with the Father and His consequent sinlessness (John 1: 1; 10: 30; 1: 18, N.E.B.).

(b) *The revelation was given by means of His character, His teaching and His work.* His sacrifice on the Cross was the supreme revelation of the love and the holiness of God (1 John 4: 9, 10).

(c) *The revelation given by Jesus Christ was proclaimed by the apostles.* In the Epistles we have a record of the way they explained the significance of the life and death of Jesus and, under the guidance of the Holy Spirit, showed how His teaching could be followed.

(d) *Jesus Christ is clearly the central figure of the Bible,* the One toward whom previous revelation pointed and from whom all later revelation proceeds (John 16: 12–14).

8. Prophecy and miracle play an important part in Bible revelation.

(a) *Prophecy is the telling forth, by God's servants, of what He revealed to them.* A *prophet* is one who delivers this message to men. He is God's man and God's messenger.

In no other religion are there teachers possessing the spiritual discernment and the moral insight of the prophets of Israel. They showed the life of the nation to be bound up with the will of God, and the future to be in His hands as Lord of history. Thus their words included an element of *prediction*, that is, the foretelling of events in the course of history.

(*b*) *A miracle is an act or mighty work of God* (Mark 6: 2), who is the source of power and with whom all things are possible. Such events need not be contrary to nature, even though (as Augustine said) they may seem ' contrary to what is known of nature '. In John's Gospel they are presented as ' signs ' which show forth the glory of God (John 2: 11, N.E.B.).

The Incarnation and Resurrection of Jesus Christ are supreme examples of the power of God. On the day of Pentecost, Peter declared that ' Jesus of Nazareth [was] a man approved of God unto you *by mighty works and wonders and signs, which God did by Him in the midst of you*, even as ye yourselves know ' (Acts 2: 22, R.V.).

Section IV. THE INSPIRATION OF THE SCRIPTURES

1. The meaning of divine inspiration.

(*a*) ' Inspiration ' literally means ' inbreathing '. By divine inspiration of the Bible we mean that special ' inbreathing ' or enabling by the Holy Spirit which God's chosen servants received. They communicated the truth thus revealed (2 Pet. 1: 21).

(*b*) The purpose of divine inspiration is to provide the message that will lead men to salvation through Jesus Christ and teach them how to love and serve God (2 Tim. 3: 15–17, N.E.B.; John 20: 31).

(*c*) Words like ' inspiration ', ' life ' and ' beauty ' have meaning only through a personal experience of what they signify. The Scriptures possess a quality which causes us to recognize them as uniquely authoritative and as a means of grace. This quality reinforces their claim to be God's word of salvation to men, and it is the testimony of one generation after another that through the Scriptures God finds the soul of man and the soul of man finds God.

2. The nature of the inspiration of the Scriptures.

(*a*) The doctrine of the inspiration of the Scriptures does not mean verbal dictation.   Such a theory leaves out of account the human element in the composition of the Scriptures—for example, differences of style and thought-forms, divergencies in accounts of the same events.   It would also involve the need to ascribe finality to stages of revelation which are incomplete.

The Holy Spirit does *not* deal with men as though they were machines; each of God's messengers retained his own powers and characteristics.   It is, therefore, clear that not all parts of the Bible are inspired in the same way or in the same degree.

(*b*) The Holy Spirit endowed His messengers with insight to interpret for our profit the events through which God disclosed His will to men.

(*c*) In translations from the original language in which the writers thought and expressed themselves, the words of the translators are different but the word of God is unchanged.   We hear His word in the various translations as surely as in the Hebrew and Greek originals.

3. Evidences that the Bible is inspired by God.

(*a*) *Internal evidence:*

(i) The remarkable unity of the Bible points to the fact that the one God must have inspired its various human authors.

Its sixty-six books were written during a period of between 1,500 and 1,600 years, and embrace almost every form of literature—law, history, parable, poetry, prophecy, proverb, biography, letters.   Its authors, about forty in number, include warriors and statesmen, kings and peasants, prophets and priests, fishermen and herdsmen.   Yet in spite of the many differences between the various books, the Bible is a unity through its testimony to the divine revelation which it both records and interprets.   Only by study of the words and thought-forms of the Old Testament is the New Testament fully intelligible. Equally the Old Testament can be understood only in the light of the New. The central theme is Jesus Christ—the Old Testament prepared for Him; the New Testament shows how He fulfilled and exceeded Old Testament expectations.

(ii) Jesus Christ frequently appealed to the Old Testament Scriptures as having divine origin and authority.

He said that the Jews were those ' unto whom the word of God came ' (John 10: 35) and He spoke of their Scriptures as ' that which was spoken unto you by God ' (Matt. 22: 31).

To them He referred His hearers, asking, ' Did ye never read in the Scriptures?' (Matt. 21: 42). He told the Jews, ' Ye do err, not knowing the Scriptures' (Matt. 22: 29). He met the tempter with ' It is written' (Matt. 4: 4, 7, 10).

Jesus Christ taught that the Old Testament Scriptures pointed forward to and were fulfilled in Himself (Luke 24: 44).

(iii) The writers of the New Testament testify to their belief in the inspiration of the Old Testament by their appeals to its authority and their quotations from its pages. For example, the Epistle to the Hebrews would be inexplicable apart from the Old Testament.

(iv) Both Testaments record the claims of many to have spoken the words given by God; some claim by His command (Exod. 34: 27; Rev. 1: 17–19). Many of the messages recorded in the Old Testament are prefaced by the words: ' Thus saith the Lord ' or similar phrases. The Apostle Paul also refers to divine inspiration (1 Cor. 2: 13).

(v) The Bible record of the transforming effect of its own

message is a testimony to its inspiration. When King Josiah ' heard the words of the book of the law . . . he rent his clothes ' (2 Kings 22: 11), and when he called the people together small and great and ' read in their ears all the words of the book ' they were so affected by its message that the king was able to carry out far-reaching reforms (2 Kings 23). Nehemiah (chapter 13) describes that when the book of Moses was read ' in the audience of the people ' they agreed to right all wrongs which had been allowed in public life.

The New Testament (Acts 8: 31–37) tells how the reading of Isa. 53, and an explanation of this passage, led to an Ethiopian's conversion, and Peter's Old Testament quotations, with his application of them to Christ, led to the conversion of thousands on the day of Pentecost. In 2 Tim. 3: 15 we read that the Holy Scriptures are able ' to make you wise and lead you to salvation ' (N.E.B.).

(b) *External evidence:*

(i) Many of the messages recorded in the Bible were spoken by men at risk of abuse or the cost of life itself. So sure were they of divine inspiration that, whatever the consequences to themselves personally, they could not refrain from uttering what was to them ' the word of the Lord ' (Jer. 20: 8, 9; Acts 7: 51–60).

(ii) Prophecy and divine promises figure in the Scriptures, and their fulfilment is testimony to their inspiration. For example, the unique history of the Jews and their survival as a race continues to be one long fulfilment of the covenant made by God with Abraham (Gen. 17: 1–8), and of the warnings uttered by their prophets as to the consequences of certain lines of conduct. The fulfilment in Jesus Christ and His Church of hopes and prophecies recorded in the Old Testament is also a powerful witness.

(iii) By their selection of the books which were finally

adopted as the Canon of Scripture, the Jewish and Christian communities recognized them as inspired (see also sect. V).

(*c*) *Experiential evidence:*

  (i) The Bible is adapted to the deepest needs of all men, and alone satisfactorily points out how these needs can be met. This supports the conclusion that God who created man also inspired the Bible.

 (ii) The Bible exerts a blessed influence upon all who accept its teaching. A large part of the world has been transformed by the standards of purity, truth, justice and mercy which have been brought to men through the Bible. Especially is this true of the teaching of Christ, who is the Bible's central figure.

(iii) The personal experience of all who accept and follow Bible teaching is, to them, convincing evidence that the Bible is inspired. Such people find that the witness of the Holy Spirit in their hearts accords with the word of God. ' I know ', they say, ' that the Bible is inspired because it inspires me.'

4. The inspiration of the Bible is sometimes challenged because of certain alleged errors and discrepancies.

To this it may be replied that:

(*a*) So-called mistakes often only *appear* to be such and disappear with a better understanding of the writer's point of view, aim, method of writing and surroundings. For instance, divergencies in parallel narratives are sometimes due to the writers' different ways of observing or describing the facts (as in the Gospels) or because the method of writing history (as in the Old Testament) was not to analyse sources or documents but to combine them.

(*b*) Discrepancies in the Bible are of minor importance—such as differences in numbers or names. They are caused largely through errors of copyists or translators during the centuries before books were printed, but do not affect vital doctrinal truths. In all that concerns our salvation, holy living and eternal welfare, the Bible can be accepted as trustworthy.

(*c*) With regard to the relationship of the Bible to science, it is a mistake to consider that the aim of the Bible is to give a history of the universe or be a textbook of human knowledge. We must avoid the error of those who regard advances in scientific *knowledge* (not theories) as inimical to the truth and authority of the Scriptures, and describe those who accept them as enemies of the faith. Instead of entering into scientific detail, the Bible sets before men great religious truths—the creation of the world by God, its dependence upon Him, His constant activity in it, and His loving care for all that He has made.

Section V. HOW OUR BIBLE CAME TO US

1. The Canon of Scripture.

' Canon ' is the transliteration of a Greek word meaning ' a measuring stick, a staff to keep things straight ', so the *Canon of Scripture* refers to the list of Old and New Testament books which the Christian Church regards as the authoritative rule of Christian faith (doctrine) and the standard of Christian practice (conduct).

The *Canon of Scripture* falls into two main divisions, known as the *Old Testament* and the *New Testament*. The *Old Testament* is the Christian term for the Jewish Scriptures, whose origin and authority lie in the covenant (testament means covenant) relationship between God and Israel instituted through Moses.

The *New Testament* is the Christian term for those writings which contain the record of the ' New Covenant ', foreshadowed in the Old Testament (Jer. 31: 31–34) and fulfilled in Jesus Christ (Mark 14: 24; Luke 22: 20). In the two words *Old* and *New* is the explanation of the Christian attitude toward the Jewish Scriptures: ' In that He saith, A new covenant, He hath made the first old ' (Heb. 8: 13) ; ' He [Jesus] is the mediator of a better covenant, which was established upon better promises ' (Heb. 8: 6). (See also 3 below.)

2. The Old Testament.

These thirty-nine books were accepted by the Jews into their Canon of Holy Scripture in three stages—the *Law*, the *Prophets* and the *Writings*. Thus Jesus spoke of things being ' fulfilled, which were written in the law of Moses, and in the prophets, and in the psalms ' (Luke 24: 44); the word ' Psalms ' in this reference representing the ' Writings ', of which group it was the first book.

(*a*) *The Law* (sometimes called the *Pentateuch* from the Greek for ' five books ') consisted of Genesis, Exodus, Leviticus, Numbers and Deuteronomy. *The Law* is generally considered to have gained canonical status by about 400 B.C. It was from these books that Ezra read to the people of Jerusalem (Neh. 8: 8; 10: 29), and it is these five books which the Samaritans possessed (with whom the Jews had ' no dealings ' after the fourth century B.C. See reference to the Samaritan Pentateuch on page 27).

(*b*) *The Prophets* consisted of the ' *Former Prophets* ' (Joshua, Judges, Samuel and Kings—which, although historical books, were included among the prophets because they disclosed the prophetic interpretation of the activity of God in history) and the ' *Latter Prophets* ' (Isaiah, Jeremiah, Ezekiel and the ' Book of the Twelve ', which declared God's will, His judgments and His actions). The ' Twelve ' (Hosea, Joel, Amos, Obadiah, Jonah, Micah, Nahum, Habakkuk, Zephaniah, Haggai, Zechariah and Malachi) are also known as ' minor prophets ', but this refers to their brevity and not to any inferiority in comparison with other prophetic writings.

Although ' the Prophets ' seem to have gained general acceptance by about 200 B.C., the existence of the two groups is evident as early as 520 B.C., for Zech. 1: 4; 7: 7 refer to the ' former prophets '. (See the definition of ' prophet ' and ' prophecy ' in sect. III, para. 8 (*a*).)

(*c*) *The Writings* consisted of a wide range of sacred literature which included poetry, history, wisdom and apocalyptic writings.

NOTE: It was not until about A.D. 90 that Jewish rabbis at the ' Council of Jamnia ' ' closed ' the Jewish Canon by limiting the

' Writings ' to Psalms, Proverbs, Job, the five rolls of Song of Songs (Song of Solomon), Ruth, Lamentations, Ecclesiastes, Esther, Daniel, Ezra, Nehemiah and Chronicles. (This is their order in the Jewish Scriptures.)

The Apocrypha (Greek for ' hidden writings ') consists of fourteen books rejected at the ' Council of Jamnia ' and so excluded from the Jewish Canon of Scripture. These books originated mostly outside of Palestine, among Greek-speaking and Greek-writing Jews in Alexandria. Because of this they eventually came to be included in the *Septuagint*, the Greek translation of the Old Testament Scriptures attributed to seventy Jewish scholars (hence the name *Septuagint*; the Roman numerals LXX are used to designate this translation) which originated in Alexandria in the third century B.C.

When Christianity spread beyond Palestine it was the *Septuagint* which was used by Greek-speaking Jewish and Gentile converts. The Early Church, therefore, automatically included the Apocrypha (as part of the *Septuagint*) in their ' Old Testament Scriptures '. The Roman Catholic Church still follows this practice as does the Eastern Orthodox Church. Since the Reformation, however, the Protestant churches have accepted the Apocrypha ' for edification, but not for doctrine '; hence its omission from the Authorized Version.

3. The Christian attitude toward the Old Testament.

While the Christian Church has always accepted and valued the Old Testament, it has followed the teaching of our Lord and the New Testament writers, who stressed the incomplete nature of its revelation. The Old Testament spoke of men's need and hope of a Saviour but, as the Epistle to the Hebrews makes clear, the New Testament is the record of their fulfilment in Jesus Christ. The Old Testament contains a progressive revelation of God, with high peaks of truth, but (as sect. III, para. 6 shows) this was but preparatory; the divine revelation everywhere culminates in Jesus Christ. Nevertheless, the Old Testament is a necessary part of our Bible; it is fundamental and preparatory to the New. As Augustine of Hippo said, the New Testament is implicit in the Old, the Old Testament is explicit in the New.

The Christian Church quickly learnt to distinguish between the moral and ceremonial elements of the Law (Acts 15). The importance of the former is clearly revealed in the moral and ethical emphasis of every New Testament writing. Jesus said of the Law, ' I did not come to abolish, but to complete ' (Matt. 5: 17, N.E.B.); Matt. 5: 17–48 goes beyond a literal or external compliance with the Law and deepens and intensifies its moral demands. For those who accepted the ' New Covenant ', the ceremonial requirements of the Mosaic Law were seen to be no longer binding. Their chief function had been to secure a right relationship with God, but in this their usefulness was limited (Heb. 9: 9, 10, N.E.B.)—hence the need admitted in the writings of the Old Testament itself for a ' New Covenant ' (Jer. 31: 31–34), and the New Testament emphasis that a justification which brings a right relationship with God is by faith in Christ alone (Rom. 3: 19–26; Eph. 2: 8, 9, 18).

The Law was impermanent; it was a ' schoolmaster ' to bring men to Christ, ' but after that faith is come, we are no longer under a schoolmaster ' (Gal. 3: 25). The ceremonial ordinances foreshadowed the truth in Christ, but the need for their continual repetition was indicative of their incomplete nature. Jesus is our great High Priest, and we are ' sanctified through the offering of the body of Jesus Christ *once for all* ' (Heb. 10: 10). Because of this, the ceremonial aspects of the Law of Moses are no longer binding; through Christ the believer can ' draw near with a true heart in full assurance of faith ' (Heb. 10: 22).

The ' Old Covenant ' called for obedience to a written code which lacked the power to produce life. The ' New Covenant ' is good news (the gospel) because it offers the believer a new relationship to God through faith in Jesus Christ, and both demands and offers enabling power to fulfil ' the law of Christ ' (Gal. 6: 2).

4. The New Testament.

Although the twenty-seven books which now comprise the

New Testament were not written to compete with or to replace the Old Testament Scriptures, the Early Church soon came to recognize them as supremely authoritative for ' Christian faith and practice '.

The *Gospels* were originally prepared to meet the need of a particular church or group of churches for written records of the life and teaching of Jesus Christ.

The *Epistles* were letters written by church leaders to counsel the young churches and their leaders on problems of faith and practice arising out of their particular situation and environment.

Collections of Gospels and Epistles were soon being made by many churches, and these were not only used in the instruction of new converts but also found an important place in church services alongside the Old Testament Scriptures.

Because many so-called ' Gospels ' and 'Acts '—allegedly of apostolic origin—became widespread, it was necessary for church leaders to define those which accorded with the Christian rule of faith. Eusebius of Caesarea, the church historian of the early fourth century A.D., divided such writings into three groups: (i) universally acknowledged, (ii) disputed, (iii) spurious and heretical. At that time he placed twenty of the present New Testament writings in the first group and seven in the second.

Such decisions were not arbitrary, but seem to have been based on three essentials: that the writing

(i) conformed to the rule of faith (or creed) handed down in the Church;

(ii) was of apostolic origin (written by or containing the teaching of the earliest apostles);

(iii) was in use in the churches.

Thus Church Councils confirmed what had already been accepted by general usage. Many writings were rejected as unauthentic—for example, some ' gospels ', such as that of Thomas, which attributed fantastic miracles to the child Jesus. Other writings, though of value, failed because lacking apostolic origin (such as the *Shepherd of Hermas*, the *Teaching of the Twelve Apostles* (the Didache), and the Epistles of *Clement* and *Barnabas*).

The earliest known orthodox Canon is the *Muratorian Canon*

(named after its eighteenth-century discoverer). This was a Latin translation of a Greek original, usually dated about A.D. 170–190. Although incomplete, the list names the four Gospels, the Acts and seventeen Epistles.

More complete is the Canon of Cyril, Bishop of Jerusalem (A.D. 340) and that of the Council of Laodicaea (A.D. 363) which list twenty-six books; only the Revelation is excluded. All the twenty-seven books now known as the New Testament are, however, listed in:

(i) the Festal Epistle of Athanasius, Bishop of Alexandria (A.D. 367);

(ii) the decisions of the Roman synod of A.D. 393;

(iii) the decisions of the Council of Hippo (A.D. 393) and the third Council of Carthage (A.D. 397), both of which were greatly influenced by Augustine, Bishop of Hippo.

It is not because these various books are in the Canon that they are authoritative; they are there because of the authority of the truth they contain.

5. The sources from which modern translations are made.

Although countless manuscripts of the Scriptures were destroyed in the great persecution of the Church under the Emperor Diocletian in the first decade of the fourth century A.D., the principal surviving Greek manuscripts of the Scriptures belong to that century. Even more significant is the fact that these manuscripts were in circulation at the time of the important Church Councils which made decisions regarding the Canon of Scripture (see para. 4 above).

Fragments of manuscripts from early periods still survive, but the earliest remaining manuscripts of considerable length are:

Codex Vaticanus (in the Vatican library), which contains both Testaments although the New is incomplete.

Codex Sinaiticus (discovered in a monastery on Mount Sinai). The greater part of the Codex, which contains much of the Old and all of the New Testament, is now in the British Museum.

Both are dated in the fourth century A.D.

Two other important codices are the *Alexandrinus* (fifth century A.D.), which contains most of both Testaments; and *Bezae* (fifth/sixth century A.D.), an incomplete copy of the Gospels and Acts.

Modern translators are able to refer not only to these and many less complete manuscripts, but to older translations in such languages as Old Latin (about A.D. 160), Syriac (about A.D. 150), Coptic, Ethiopic and Gothic (fourth century A.D.) and Armenian (fifth century A.D.). They can also refer to surviving copies of commentaries by church scholars of the early centuries, as well as other manuscripts and papyri that help to clarify the meaning of unusual words and phrases. Comparison of manuscripts helps scholars to discover the original text and to eliminate the glosses (added comments) and errors of copyists.

Although the Dead Sea Scrolls, discovered in recent years, have included copies of some Old Testament writings which can be dated in the pre-Christian era, *Hebrew* manuscripts of the Old Testament are generally of later date. The American Revised Standard Version of the Old Testament (1952) made use of such ancient versions as the Septuagint Greek, the Samaritan Hebrew Pentateuch, the Syriac, and the Latin Vulgate. Reference was also made to such Jewish books as the Targums.

The establishment of the original Hebrew and Aramaic text of the Old Testament is difficult, but basic for translation is the important consonantal Hebrew and Aramaic text as fixed early in the Christian era and revised by Jewish scholars (the ' Masoretes ') of the sixth to ninth centuries A.D.

6. The division of the text of Scripture into chapters and verses was adopted by the sixteenth century.

3

GOD

' We believe there is only one God, who is infinitely perfect—the Creator, Preserver and Governor of all things—and who is the only proper object of religious worship ' (Article 2).

' We believe that there are three persons in the Godhead—the Father, the Son and the Holy Ghost—undivided in essence and co-equal in power and glory ' (Article 3).

Section I.   INTRODUCTION

These two Articles are taken together because they have one main subject—the being and attributes of God.   In particular they set forth that God is

(a) of infinite perfection in power and glory;

(b) the Creator, Preserver and Governor of all;

(c) alone to be regarded and treated as God (' the only proper object of religious worship ');

(d) One, yet Three in One.

In addition to what is said in these two Articles, teaching about God is found in each of the other nine.

Two further preliminary observations may be made, the first of which is that finite man cannot fully know the infinite God (Isa. 46: 5; 1 Tim. 6: 15, 16).   Indeed, man's knowledge of God is limited to what it has pleased God to reveal of Himself.   Such knowledge, even when disclosed, has to be expressed of necessity in human terms, none of which is sufficient for the task.

Nevertheless, the second point is that God desires that men should know Him.   The Word became flesh (John 1: 14).   He whom no man has seen at any time was made known by One in whom ' dwelleth all the fulness of the Godhead bodily ' (Col. 2: 9). This revelation has been given so that men might respond in loving obedience to Him who thus made Himself known as holy love.

Section II.   THE ATTRIBUTES OF GOD

1. The subject matter of this section.

The Statement of Doctrine uses the word ' essence ' (' un-divided in essence '), a word which means ' the distinctive nature of anything, that which makes it what it is '.

In the Bible there are many statements about the qualities which mark the distinctive nature of God. These are called His attributes and the declarations concerning them serve three purposes:

(*a*) *They show that He has powers and qualities which belong to Him alone.*

(*b*) *They give to men convincing reasons why they should regard Him with reverence yet with trust.*

(*c*) *They help to correct mistaken ideas men may have about God.*

Some of these attributes have to do with the unique nature of His being; some are statements about His powers; some have to do with qualities which in man would be called moral virtues.

Such an analysis as the above is a concession to human thought; the nature of God is indivisible and His attributes are all inter-related.

2. Attributes specially concerned with the unique nature of God's being.

(*a*) *He is personal*, that is to say, He is not to be thought of as a power, or an influence, or as being some *thing*. Throughout the Bible He is shown to be some *One* who is personal and, as our Father, fulfils all that is implied by this relationship to man (see sect. V. 2(*c*)).

The creature cannot be more personal than the Creator. The Bible asks:

> Shall the thing framed say of him that framed it, he had no understanding? (Isa. 29: 16).

> He that planted the ear, shall He not hear? ... He that teacheth man knowledge, shall not He know? (Ps. 94: 9, 10).

(b) *He is spirit.*

He is not to be thought of as having bodily form.

This does not make Him any the less real, for He is the living God, the Source and Lord of all things. When Jesus said ' God is spirit ', He was teaching that God is free from the limitations of time and space and can be approached by worshipping hearts everywhere (John 4: 21–24, N.E.B.).

When the Bible speaks of God's ' ears ', ' eyes ', ' mouth ', ' hand ' and ' arm ', it is conveying in symbolic fashion the truth that God acts with those powers which in man are effective only by these physical means.

(c) *He is eternal and self-existent* (Ps. 90: 2).

As the Eternal God He has neither beginning nor ending. He is self-existent and all-sufficient, which means that His being and powers are not derived from, nor are dependent on, any source outside of Himself.

His eternal self-existence is expressed simply yet profoundly by the divine declaration, ' I am ', and by man in the statement, ' God is '.

(d) *He is unchanging* (Jas. 1: 17).

This attribute is one aspect of the perfection of God, for any change could be a movement only to imperfection. God's unchangeableness is not like the rigidity of a machine, but is the attribute of a person whose nature, while unchanging, finds expression in an infinite variety of ways.

(e) *He alone is God* (Isa. 45: 5).

This statement about God refers to His supremacy. He is above all; there is nothing outside the scope of His rule.

(f) *He is One yet Three-in-One.*

This doctrine is dealt with in sect. V.

3. Attributes concerned with God's power.

(*a*) *He is everywhere present* (*omnipresent*) (Jer. 23: 23, 24).

(*b*) *He is all-knowing* (*omniscient*) (Ps. 147: 5; Heb. 4: 13).

In terms of *understanding*, this means that nothing is mystery to Him; in terms of *awareness*, that no event is hidden from His consciousness.

This awareness is more than the experience of a *seeing* God, who as Governor of all 'searcheth the hearts' (Rom. 8: 27); it is the experience of the God who is aware of His own acts as Creator and Preserver of all. His knowledge is total for, in addition to knowing Himself (1 Cor. 2: 11), He knows the creation He controls (Luke 12: 6, 7).

Yet there is more. This omniscience is of One who 'inhabiteth eternity' (Isa. 57: 15) and is free from the restrictions imposed by the time pattern which compels human knowledge to move from a known present and past to an unknown future. So, with regard to past and present, God is all-knowing, and also knows all the possibilities of the future (Isa. 46: 9, 10).

Infinity and eternity are beyond the conditions of space and time wherein man dwells. God is Lord of eternity and of time. Time is His servant and not His master. God uses time. His acts, which invade human experience, of necessity appear to man in a time pattern as historical events, although without losing their eternal and timeless value. But God Himself is above time and is free from the compulsions of time (2 Pet. 3: 8; Ps. 90: 4).

Man, who lives in space and time, cannot understand the experience of God, who is not subject to these conditions. It would not be necessary to discuss this had not emphasis on God's omniscience led some Christian thinkers to deny man's free will (see chap. 7, sect. V, paras. 2 and 3).

(*c*) *He is almighty* (*omnipotent*) (Gen. 17: 1; Isa. 26: 4; Matt. 19: 26; Rev. 19: 6).

God's omnipotence means that there is no boundary to His power. He can do all He wills to do, but all He does is in accord with His nature. He cannot deny Himself. He ' worketh all things after the counsel of His own will ' (Eph. 1: 11).

This means more than the statement that God is able. His was the power at work in creation and all power possessed by created things is derived from Him. If God ceased to be, there would be no being anywhere. The greatest expression of His power known to man is that of redemption.

As God's omnipotence is bound up with all His other attributes all things are therefore within the compass of His presence, His knowledge and His power.

4. Attributes which show the moral excellencies of the divine nature.

(a) *He is holy* (Lev. 11: 44 and 1 Pet. 1: 16; Matt. 6: 9; Ps. 145: 17).

This attribute of holiness has three effects:

   (i) It indicates the awesomeness of God and calls for a corresponding reverence in man.

   (ii) It manifests itself negatively as abhorrence of and separation from all that is evil, and positively as delight in all that is good.

   (iii) It communicates itself to everyone whom God possesses and uses, for all holiness has its source in His holiness.

(b) *He is love* (1 John 4: 8).

This attribute is revealed

   (i) in the active goodwill God shows to all as Preserver of His creation (Ps. 145: 9), to the evil and the good, the just and the unjust (Matt. 5: 45);

   (ii) in His condemnation of all forms of self-seeking—the antithesis of love; and

   (iii) most of all in His work of redemption.

The love of God is unique; it has a quality distinct from human love and earthly experience can provide no adequate comparison for it. We are therefore dependent on divine revelation not only for the truth that God is love, but also for the explanation of what this means. For this reason the declaration ' God is love ' must always be interpreted in terms of what that love does. For example:

> God is love. In this was manifested the love of God toward us, because that God sent His only begotten Son into the world, that we might live through Him. Herein is love, not that we loved God, but that He loved us, and sent His Son to be the propitiation for our sins (1 John 4: 8-10).

Moreover, this redeeming act is to be seen as an expression of the constant attitude of God to man, an attitude that always seeks man's highest good. Nor was the divine love diminished or halted by man's sins, for it was ' while we were yet sinners, Christ died for us ', and ' when we were enemies, we were reconciled to God by the death of His Son ' (Rom. 5: 8, 10). The love of God shines most strongly when most severely tested.

Thus it is wrong to regard God's love as an evidence of His approval of a man's character and conduct, or to say that He does not love those of whose spiritual condition He may disapprove.

Further, God's love is not rightly understood unless seen in unity with the divine holiness.

His is a holy love, each attribute being the crowning glory of the other. The glory of God's holiness is that His moral perfection is expressed in love, and the glory of His love is that it is always manifested in harmony with His holiness.

The high objective of God for man is found in 1 John 3: 1-3:

> Behold, what manner of love the Father hath bestowed upon us, that we should be called the sons of God. . . . Beloved, now are we the sons of God, and it doth not yet appear what we shall be: but we know that, when He shall appear, we shall be like Him; for we shall see Him as He is. And every man that hath this hope in him purifieth himself, even as He is pure.

Because this is the action of holy love, here is both a gift to be received (vv. 1, 2) and a searching requirement to be met (v. 3).

Section III. GOD AS THE CREATOR, PRESERVER AND GOVERNOR OF ALL THINGS

(See Gen. 1: 1; Isa. 45: 12; Rom. 11: 36, N.E.B.).

1. The words 'The Creator, Preserver and Governor of all things' should be considered first of all in their association with one another and in their relation to the complete Statement of Doctrine.

(*a*) The complete phrase teaches that God is not only the uncaused Cause of all that exists apart from Himself, but that His creation remains in His hands, subject to His government and dependent on Him for its continued existence.

Whenever one of the three words, ' Creator ', ' Preserver ', ' Governor ', is being used, the other two need to be borne in mind. Together they indicate that the universe is not meaningless but that there is a purpose in creation, and that in this purpose is to be found the answer to the question as to why creation took place at all. Likewise, the manner of the divine operation in preservation and government is rightly understood only when it is seen in the light of this purpose.

The words ' Preserver ' and ' Governor ' should always be linked for men are at times too ready to welcome God as Preserver but to reject Him as Governor.

(*b*) This phrase also includes what should be said about the relationship of God to man. God is the Preserver and Governor of things spiritual as well as of things material, and thus is known not only in the relationship of Creator of His creatures, but as Father acting in wisdom, holiness and love.

(*c*) The words ' all things ' refer to the total universe—to things ' that are in heaven, and that are in earth, visible and invisible ' (Col. 1: 16).

2. As Creator, God has, by His will, brought into existence everything there is apart from Himself.

(*a*) The natural sciences explore the part of creation available to human investigation and thereby discover the manner of its working and the treasure it contains, but God is the reason both for its existence and for its characteristic nature. He remains the origin of all that science has discovered and may yet discover.

(b) It may be, as some think, that adaptation in nature came about largely by evolution; but even if that be so, evolution is simply a *method* by which nature works. Behind it there is still needed an intelligent Being having the power to cause it to work in that or any other particular way.

(c) God is active within this creation, yet is distinct from it. He is also over it. The special revelation He has given declares that He has purposes concerning it which are not yet fully realized.

3. Despite the fact that God is Creator, we have to recognize the presence of evil in His creation.

(a) The presence of evil in its many and varied forms provokes two great challenges to the declarations of this Article:

(i) If God is the Creator of all, do evil things also owe their origin to this ' infinitely perfect ' Being?

(ii) If He is Governor of all, and is credited with almighty power and a declared purpose to reign in righteousness, do not existing conditions deny such a claim?

(b) These are proper questions to ask. They relate to the crucial part of the Christian message. Such matters as God's utter antagonism to evil, His supremacy in spite of its existence, and His action to expel it from His Kingdom, are among the main themes of the Bible. Their importance in The Salvation Army's Statement of Doctrine is seen in the fact that the existence of evil in God's world and His action against it become the one subject with which all the other Articles are concerned (see the survey of the eleven Articles, chap. 1, sect. II).

For this reason the two questions outlined above need only be raised here, for the brief answer to the presence of evil in creation is that the evil was not created by God, and that it has no place in His ideal Kingdom (Gen. 1: 31).

As a responsible moral being man possesses a free will which he can assert against the will of God, whose government allows for disobedience and its consequences. The divine government of men is not that of a Ruler who in detached enthronement compels obedience by the exercise of irresistible power, but that of a Father who constrains by the power of a seeking, saving love. Holy love is the only atmosphere in which free spirits can both retain their freedom and yet worthily obey.

4. God is Preserver of all things.

(a) *He preserves the whole of creation by His power* (Isa. 40: 25, 26).

(b) *His preservation includes provision for life and its maintenance* (Gen. 8: 22; Ps. 145: 9, 15, 16; Acts 17: 25, 28).

(c) *His provision is not withheld from those who rebel against His will* (Matt. 5: 44, 45).

(d) *This provision requires man's co-operation for its use and development.*

God is not to be thought of as an unfailing Provider who saves the indolent and careless from the result of their neglect. Their impoverishment arises, not from His failure, but from theirs (Prov. 6: 6-11; 2 Thess. 3: 10).

Furthermore, God's law in these matters lays upon man the obligation lovingly to care for the needy, as being one of the ways in which he can display a likeness to his Maker (1 John 3: 16, 17). The scriptural comment concerning those whose needs remain unrelieved is that this is not because they have been forgotten by God, but because they have been wronged or forgotten by man (Isa. 3: 14, 15; Matt. 25: 42-45).

(e) *This divine care is seen in the light of the greatest provision of all, the offer of salvation* (2 Pet. 3: 9). While all men need bread no man lives by bread alone. Spiritual needs take priority (Matt. 6: 33).

(f) *Those who through living in obedience to the law of God's Kingdom are exposed to opposition and suffering, He regards with special tenderness and enables them to triumph in and over adversity* (Ps. 121: 7; Rom. 8: 32, 37).

5. God is Governor of all things.

(*a*) *He rules over creation* by means of ' natural law '.

(*b*) *He rules over man*, who as a creature is subject to ' natural law '. As a child of God he is subject also to the law of the Kingdom. This includes the moral law, from whose claims, although they may be disregarded, there is no final escape.

Section IV.   GOD AS THE ONLY PROPER OBJECT OF RELIGIOUS WORSHIP

1. The foundation of this doctrine is that God is the only proper object of religious worship because He alone is God (Exod. 20: 3; Ps. 96: 5, 8, 9; Matt. 4: 10).

(*a*) Religious worship is here regarded as divine worship, and this is a sign that the worshipper regards the object of his worship to be divine.

The words ' who is the only proper object of religious worship ' not only give additional knowledge but affirm that knowledge must affect practice.

Although no word is given about the exact form of worship we should use, this principle allows for diverse forms of worship, so long as all are directed to God and appropriate to His holiness and majesty.

(*b*) The commandment ' Thou shalt have no other gods before Me ' did not *introduce* religion and worship to men; it was an attempt to *correct* already existing religious ideas and practices. Whenever man has become persuaded that his affairs were being controlled by some higher power, he has made some attempt to come into a relationship with that power, the nature and quality of his response being determined by his ideas of the character of the object to which his worship has been directed.

Man is a worshipping creature, and if his capacity for seeking the highest and the unseen is not directed to God, it will be given to some lesser object. The condemnation of such action is not only that it dishonours God but that it injures the worshipper. A revealing presentation of the effects of depraved worship is to be found in Rom. 1: 18–32.

Thus the teaching given in the First Commandment was used by Moses and succeeding prophets, then by Jesus and by the apostles and their successors, to transform and reform the worship of men.

(c) Obviously great numbers of people do not worship the true and living God. Obligation to witness is therefore laid upon those who do. How shall non-worshippers ' believe in Him of whom they have not heard? and how shall they hear without a preacher? '

The underlying principle is outlined in Rom. 10: 12–17, and seen in action in Acts 14: 15–17 and Acts 17: 22–31.

(d) When the teaching of this phrase is applied to those who profess to be believers, it condemns and corrects all aspects of inadequate and unworthy worship, such as

> (i) when worship is wholly absorbed in its own activities;
>
> (ii) when the worship due to God is transferred in whole or in part to some other object.

This failure to distinguish between creature and Creator leads to the elevation of holy places, objects, institutions or persons to a dignity to which they have no claim, and eventually to a point where they receive adoration as though they themselves are the *source* of blessings which are solely derived from God.

The New Testament contains examples of attempts to correct this error: Acts 3: 11, 12; 10: 25, 26; 14: 13–15; Rev. 22: 8, 9.

The command that nothing must be given the place that belongs to God alone is extended in the New Testament to practices and attitudes which are described as being ' idolatrous ', although having no connection with the worship of a graven image (Col. 3: 5, N.E.B.; Matt. 6: 24).

2. The religious worship spoken of here is concerned with the moral perfection of God, as well as with the doctrine that He alone is God.

(a) *A worshipful response to all that is known about Him will include*

    (i) reverence for His Deity;

    (ii) acknowledgment of Him as Creator and Preserver;

    (iii) submission to Him as Governor;

    (iv) adoration of Himself for His goodness.

(b) *The highest form of worship is when God is honoured for what He is*, without petition for benefits other than that of communion with Him.

This is a quality of worship that is evoked from man when he thinks of the goodness of God and realizes that what he most deeply admires has its source and fullest expression in Him. Man's response is then not only ' Thou art God ', but ' Thou art *worthy*, O Lord, to receive glory and honour and power '.

(c) *God calls forth worship from man on two levels :*

    (i) His command saves men from misdirecting their worship.

    (ii) His self-revelation inspires, elevates and perfects man's worship when the command is obeyed.

3. Worship, in its widest sense, involves the total response of a person to God.

Other portions of the Statement of Doctrine show that such responses as faith, repentance, full obedience and self-dedication are also required, together with the greatest response of all: ' Thou shalt love the Lord thy God with all thine heart, and with all thy soul, and with all thy might.'

Section V.   THE TRINITY

' *We believe that there are three persons in the Godhead—the Father, the Son and the Holy Ghost—undivided in essence and co-equal in power and glory* ' (Article 3).

1. Here is the doctrine of the triune nature of God.

This is a distinctively Christian doctrine unknown apart from New Testament revelation. While teaching that there is only one God (Mark 12: 29; 1 Cor. 8: 4), this revelation declares that God is Three-in-One—a Tri-unity or Trinity. Throughout the Christian Church belief in this doctrine is expressed in words closely similar to those used in Article 3.

2. The basic truths presented by this Statement about the Father, the Son and the Holy Spirit* are:

(a) *There is distinction between the Three.* The titles Father, Son and Holy Spirit are not shared or interchangeable.

(b) *Father, Son and Holy Spirit are, nevertheless, inseparably One.* The three Persons are ' undivided in essence ', essence being a word which stands for the wholeness of the divine nature. God is Father, Son and Holy Spirit.

(c) *Father, Son and Holy Spirit are, therefore, each fully divine.* They co-equally share *divine* power and *divine* glory, so that it is correct to speak of God the Father, of God the Son and of God the Holy Spirit.

The word ' person ' as applied to the Godhead was the nearest English word for a Greek term introduced into doctrine in order to emphasize that the three Persons are not to be thought of as a part, a phase, or no more than an activity of God. No language can supply an exact word to fulfil all that is required in this connection, for a unique fact demands a unique word.

Inasmuch as the Father, the Son and the Holy Spirit are One, the current meaning of the word ' person ', as describing an individual who is separate from others, reveals the inadequacy of the word to meet the full requirement of the doctrine. In face of transcendent mystery all we can say is that the Father is personal, the Son is personal, the Holy Spirit is personal—yet they are not three but one Person (see also chaps. 4 and 5).

* The variations in the use of the terms ' Holy Ghost ' (in Article 3) and ' Holy Spirit ' (in Article 7) have no doctrinal significance.

The two forms of expression have been taken from the Authorized Version of the English Bible, where the same Greek word is translated in some places by the word ' Ghost ' and in other places by the word ' Spirit '. It is preferable to use the latter form. At the time when this translation was made (A.D. 1611) the word ' Ghost ' had a meaning that has not been retained in modern usage. There is nothing vague or unreal about the Spirit of God. He is the Spirit of power, ' the Lord and giver of life '.

3. The doctrine of the Trinity cannot be studied without reference to the means by which these truths about God were revealed to men.

Men learned of the triune nature of God by experience and history before they began to formulate the doctrine itself. The doctrine of the Trinity unites three culminating aspects of the progressive revelation that God has given of Himself to man:

(a) *That which came to Israel* and is enshrined in the Old Testament record—there is only one God, the Lord of creation, who in the days to come would make a greater manifestation of His presence and power than He had done in the past.

(b) *That which came by Jesus,* when the Jewish hopes of a Messiah were fulfilled in terms beyond their highest expectation. Those who responded to this light and came to accept Jesus as truly and properly God and truly and properly man also came to believe that:

(i) although distinct from the Father who sent Him, Jesus was one with God in a Father-Son relationship;

(ii) there is Another who would later take His place but as God *within* them—the Holy Spirit, as distinct from the Father and the Son as the Son is distinct from the Father, yet *one* with Them;

(iii) these truths were part of the divine work of salvation, which could be fulfilled only through the ministry of the Son and of the Spirit.

(c) *That which came to the early disciples at Pentecost* when their experience of God indwelling became as real to them as had been their experience of God incarnate. This fulfilled the promise given by Jesus.

Under the influence of these acts of God they were brought to give divine worship to Father, Son and Spirit, yet with the clear conviction that they were worshipping one God, the God of their fathers, who had revealed Himself to men in this unexpected yet fulfilling way. (See in their context such verses as Acts 2: 33, 36; 5: 30–32; 7: 55–57, 59, 60; 15: 28.)

Thus Christian believers, knowing God to be Creator, incarnate in Jesus and specially present as the Holy Spirit in the hearts of His people, were compelled to expand their understanding of the unity of God in order to express the full significance of this progressive revelation. Eventually there emerged the doctrine of the triune nature of God, although the credal statement now widely accepted was not introduced until well after the period of Christian history covered by the New Testament record.

4. These three advancing steps in the development of the doctrine of the Trinity are reflected in the way in which the subject is presented in the eleven Articles.

(*a*) *The doctrine of the Trinity is a salvation doctrine both in its origin and in its purpose.*

> (i) By the redeeming acts of God it became known to man (see para. 3(*b*) above).

> (ii) Without the truths embodied in the doctrine of the Trinity and of the Incarnate Son, the gospel can be neither proclaimed nor received.
>
> ' The grace of the Lord Jesus Christ, and the love of God, and the communion of the Holy Ghost ' is much more than a benediction the Church receives; it is the secret of its existence.
>
> Men need to know that the ministry of the Son and the ministry of the Holy Spirit in the work of salvation are truly acts of God. They are works in which He is fully expressing His divine nature.

It is this aspect of the doctrine of the Trinity that has prominence in our Articles of Faith. Articles 4 and 6–10 are concerned with the ministry of the Son and of the Holy Spirit in bringing the salvation of God to man, while Article 3 supports and strengthens them by showing that this work is the direct action of God Himself.

(*b*) *The revelation of the eternal Deity of the Son and of the Holy Spirit teaches that the Trinity is associated with every divine act.*

The Scriptures make it clear that God the Father, God the Son, and God the Holy Spirit are equally involved in creation, preservation, government and revelation as well as in redemption.

(*c*) *The final step was taken when the doctrine of the Trinity was related to the Being of God as well as to the acts of God.*

This aspect of the doctrine is presented in Article 3, which speaks of God as He is by virtue of His own nature.

5. It is impossible adequately to picture, by means of material things, the complete truth concerning the mystery of the Godhead.

However, through the centuries imperfect analogies have been employed to serve as illustrations of the triune nature of God, such as:

(*a*) *One thing composed of three parts:* the *trefoil* (the family of plants whose leaves are formed by the union of three leaflets); *human personality* with its powers of mind, feeling and will; *man* consisting of body, soul and spirit.

(*b*) *One thing which has three forms or states of experience: water* existing as ice, liquid and vapour; *man sustaining varied relationships* being at one and the same time son, husband and father; *aspects of human self-consciousness,* in which a person using the power of knowing, is both the knower and the known; *human communication* in which there is the revealer, the thing revealed and the process of revelation.

6. Scriptural teaching related to the doctrine of the Trinity is abundant.

Jesus is the supreme source of revelation of the truths expressed in this doctrine. They are disclosed to men

(*a*) *By the teaching concerning Him:*
  (i) *In connection with His birth* (Luke 1 : 35).
  (ii) *At His baptism* (Matt. 3: 16, 17).

(iii) *In the words of John the Baptist,* which show the significance of the baptism of Jesus and its connection with Pentecost (John 1 : 33).

(iv) *In the messages of the apostles,* who also saw in the Old Testament certain passages which could be used in support of those truths fully disclosed in Christ—such as Acts 2: 34; Heb. 1 : 8, 9.

(b) *By what Jesus said Himself.*

The promises of Jesus at the Last Supper (John, chaps. 13–16) are seen to have been fulfilled, and His prayers (John 17) are seen to have been answered, in the Acts and in the Epistles:

(i) *In the coming of spiritual life to men and the coming into being of the Church* (Acts 2: 32, 33; 2 Thess. 2: 13; 1 Pet. 1 : 2).

(ii) *In bringing and confirming to men the message of salvation* (Heb. 2: 3, 4).

(iii) *In the work of the Atonement and its effects* (Eph. 2: 18; Titus 3: 5, 6).

(iv) *In indwelling power* (Eph. 3: 14–17).

(v) *In the equipping of His servants for work and witness* (1 Cor. 12: 4–6).

7. The form of language used in stating this doctrine is linked with the Church of the third to fifth centuries, when there was special need to safeguard Christian faith against three forms of error concerning the Trinity.

(a) These errors were:

(i) That in the Godhead there is no *distinction* of persons, that Father, Son and Spirit are nothing more than three aspects of one Person, that God appears sometimes as Father, sometimes as Son, and sometimes as Spirit.

(ii) That Father, Son and Spirit have such complete distinction that there are three Gods.

(iii) That there is no Trinity, in that neither Son nor Spirit are truly divine.

(*b*) This Article deals with the first error by saying, ' There are three persons in the Godhead '; with the second that the Three are ' undivided in essence '; and with the third by saying that the Three are ' co-equal in power and glory '.

8. An essential part of this doctrine is that there are aspects in which the Three-in-One are also distinct from one another.

(*a*) The titles God the Father, God theSon and God the Holy Spirit are distinctive. The order in which these appear in Article 3 is also a mark of distinction between the Three, for it follows the established practice which names the Father as the First Person, the Son as the Second Person, and the Spirit as the Third Person of the Trinity.

(*b*) The Father is presented as the First Person because He is the fount or source from which all else derives.

The supreme reason why He is called Father is that He is such in the relationship of the Trinity. He is Father in relation to Son. In a unique sense He is the ' Father of our Lord Jesus Christ ', the ' Father Everlasting '.

This relationship of Fatherhood is expressed toward mankind in two ways:

(i) He is the Father of all men, in that they are His creatures and the objects of His providential care (Eph. 4: 6).

(ii) In a more intimate sense He is Father to those who are adopted into the family of God through believing on the Son (John 1: 12; Rom. 8: 15).

(*c*) The Second Person, the Son, is the only begotten of the Father, specially manifested to men in the divine acts of the Incarnation and the Atonement (the subjects of Articles 4 and 6).

(*d*) The Third Person is the Holy Spirit, who is specially manifested in the work of regeneration, sanctification and the equipping of God's people for service (see chap. 5).

(*e*) It is important to note that while one Person may appear to be specially concerned in a particular divine act, the whole Godhead is involved in all divine operations. For example, ' God was in Christ, reconciling the world unto Himself ' (2 Cor. 5: 19), and the indwelling of the Spirit is in the power of ' the fulness of God ' (Eph. 3: 16–19).

(*f*) The relationship in unity of the Three who bear these distinguishing titles, is expressed by referring to the Son as being eternally *begotten* of the Father (John 3: 16), and to the Spirit as eternally *proceeding* from the Father and the Son (Acts 2: 33).

9. The word ' God ' is most frequently used for the Trinity considered as one, and for the First Person in the Trinity.

When speaking of the Son or the Spirit, the Person indicated is usually named; for instance, ' God the Son ', or ' the Son of God '; ' God the Holy Spirit ', or ' the Spirit of God '.

Prayer is addressed, sometimes to the Son or the Holy Spirit, but usually to the Father, in the name of the Son, through the Holy Spirit.

10. From this we learn that the right way to approach the doctrine of the Trinity is:

(*a*) *By following in the steps taken by those to whom it was first disclosed.* We cannot begin to understand the doctrine of the Trinity until the root teachings from which it is derived have been considered—that there is one God, the Father is God, the Son is God, the Holy Spirit is God. There is distinction between the Three yet They are One. This means that the related teaching in chaps. 4 and 5 is an essential part of the subject.

(*b*) *By seeing the doctrine in its relation to the gospel message*—that we may know the nature of the God who saves, that salvation is basically His own act, that He moves towards man in terms of *personal* encounter in all the fulness of the divine Being.

(c) *By recognizing that God does not lose His mystery in His self-revealing*. The introductory words of this chapter have special application here. We do not and cannot know all about God; human language is inadequate to state what is known, and nowhere in creation can we find anything to which He can be likened.

4

JESUS CHRIST

' We believe that in the person of Jesus Christ the divine and human natures are united; so that He is truly and properly God, and truly and properly man ' (Article 4).

Section I. INTRODUCTION

1. This statement concerning the person of Jesus Christ should be considered in its relation to the rest of the doctrine.

There is a close connection with His mission to men, the subject of Articles 6–10.

In addition, the statement that ' He is truly and properly God ' unites this Article with Articles 2 and 3, for this truth includes the Christian doctrine of the Incarnation (from the Latin word ' *carnis* ', which means ' flesh '), as stated in John 1: 14, ' The Word was made flesh, and dwelt among us '.

2. Thus in the Bible these two essential truths are set forth.

He who was manifested in the body,
vindicated in the spirit,
seen by angels;
who was proclaimed among the nations,
believed in throughout the world,
glorified in high heaven
(1 Tim. 3: 16, N.E.B.).

(*a*) *There is the record of Jesus Christ in His earthly life*—of His birth, His work and teaching, His words and deeds, His death, resurrection and ascension. These matters form the content of the Gospels.

(*b*) *There is the record which sets these events in the light of eternity*, proclaiming the Lord Jesus Christ as the incarnate Son of God, fulfilling by His mission the saving purposes of God.

Although indications of this aspect of the doctrine are found in the first three Gospels, it is more fully set forth in the other books of the New Testament—in a condensed form in such passages as Phil. 2: 6–11, but most concisely in the words spoken by Jesus to His disciples as recorded in the Fourth Gospel (John 16: 28), and in the prayer to His Father (John 17: 4, 5).

(*c*) *The doctrine of the Person of Christ must therefore be comprehensive enough to present One* ' *which is, and which was, and which is to come* ' (*Rev.* 1: 4), *and must include the truths that:*

(i) His divine nature is eternal. In the beginning He was with God and was God, active in divine works (John 1: 1–4).

(ii) By His Incarnation He became man, being born of the Virgin Mary by the power of the Holy Spirit, living on earth as a man amongst men. Yet though ' truly and properly man ' He was as ' truly and properly God '.

(iii) Because of this He could make an offering of Himself as the divine Atonement (Article 6).

(iv) His identification of Himself with man did not terminate with the Ascension. In His glorified Being He is still *one* with mankind, acting as Saviour of men by virtue of His Incarnation and accomplished Atonement (Articles 7–10; 1 Tim. 2: 5; Heb. 2: 11).

(v) He is to be made manifest to men again in divine Glory (' the coming of our Lord Jesus Christ '; Article 10).

(vi) He who ' *has appeared* once and for all at the climax of history to abolish sin by the sacrifice of Himself ', and who has entered ' heaven itself, *to appear now* before God on our behalf ', ' *will appear* a second time, sin done away, to bring salvation to those who are watching for Him ' (Heb. 9: 26, 24, 28, N.E.B.).

(*d*) *There is a unity in these statements* which means that no aspect can be considered in isolation from the rest. The truth about the person of Jesus Christ cannot be stated without reference to His mission, and the true significance of His mission cannot be declared without reference to His nature.

Section II. HIS MANHOOD

1. In the human aspect of His being He is truly and properly man (Heb. 2: 16–18).

(*a*) *Here is declared the reality of the Incarnation,* contradicting any idea that the Eternal Son ' made in the likeness of men ' was not really human, but simply appeared to be human. That such errors arose in New Testament times is clearly shown in 1 John 4: 2, 3.

(*b*) *In His earthly condition Jesus was truly man because it was divinely intended that He should be so.* For the fulfilling of the divine purpose He ' had to be made like these brothers of His in every way ' (Heb. 2: 17, N.E.B.).

Intimations of the unique nature of His person were, however, given to certain individuals (see Matt. 1: 19–21; 2: 2; Luke 2: 13–17; 2: 28–33) and later the people generally were confronted by the arresting facts of His claims and deeds. These evidences that here was no ordinary man evoked explanations of a widely differing nature (for example, Matt. 16: 13–16; John 3: 2; 7: 40–43), but none departed from the conviction that Jesus was a *man*, however extraordinary His actions and words might be.

(*c*) *The New Testament witnesses to this truth:*

(i) *Jesus spoke of Himself as being man* (John 8: 40).

(ii) *John the Baptist and the apostles did so even when speaking of His dignity and glory* (John 1: 30; Acts 2: 22; 13: 38; Rom. 1: 3).

2. The New Testament shows that Jesus was subject to all the limitations of human existence, using for His life and development only such resources as are available to man.

This is seen in the physical, emotional, mental, social, moral and spiritual aspects of His being.

(*a*) *He possessed a human body*, capable of ordinary physical sensations. He *hungered* (Mark 11: 12), *ate* (Mark 2: 16), *thirsted* (John 19: 28), was *wearied* (John 4: 6), *slept* (Matt. 8: 24), *wept* (John 11: 35) and *died* (John 19: 30).

(*b*) *The experiences of life drew from Him the normal human responses.* He manifested delight and grief, approval and disapproval, tenderness and anger, in ways and for reasons that we can understand (see Mark 1: 40, 41; 3: 1–6; 9: 33–37; 10: 21, 22; 14: 33–36—using only one Gospel). He spoke of the things that moved Him to pity, and of the things that aroused His anger and rebuke (see Luke 13: 10–17; also the parable teaching—the Unforgiving Servant in Matt. 18: 21–35, the Good Samaritan in Luke 10: 29–37 and the Prodigal Son in Luke 15: 11–32).

(*c*) *As His body was human, so also His mind was human.*

   (i) *His mind developed gradually.* In his youth He ' increased in wisdom and stature ' (Luke 2: 52).

   (ii) *He learned facts as we do.* He came seeking figs on a tree, and found none (Mark 11: 12, 13). When He wished to feed a crowd in the desert, He inquired of His disciples what food was available (Mark 6: 38; 8: 5). He asked the sisters of Lazarus, ' Where have ye laid him? ' (John 11: 34).

   (iii) *He experienced surprise*—which can be felt only by those whose knowledge is subject to limitations. He ' marvelled ' at the faith of the centurion (Matt. 8: 10), and at the unbelief of His own townsfolk (Mark 6: 6).

(*d*) *As a man He was involved in the life of the community*, affected for better or worse by the legacy of the past and by the action of contemporaries.

51

In this setting He was enriched by the benefits of His Jewish inheritance and by the blessings of home life and human friendship.

He was not immune from the economic and the political disabilities of His people as they were reflected in community life subject to some of the harsher aspects of despotic Roman and local government. Nor was He exempt from attack by those who had the intent and the power to do Him injury.

He lived as do others, as a human being in a human historic situation.

(e) *In the moral and spiritual aspects of life He was ' in all points tempted like as we are '* (Heb. 4: 15).

The Gospels record His temptations in the wilderness at the beginning of His public ministry, but also show that He was subject to spiritual conflict up to the hour of His death. To His disciples He said, ' Ye are they which have continued with Me in My temptations ' (Luke 22: 28), but even this comfort was denied Him in His final need.

The words ' in all points ' go to the root of the matter, for all temptation is basically a conflict between God's will and self-will. All men are thus tempted though not of necessity by the same form of enticement. The nature of temptation will vary with the nature and the circumstances of the one who is tempted. But the root choice which Jesus had to make (Mark 14: 36) was between the pressure of His own desires and the will of God for Him. In this He is one with us.

(f) *In His spiritual life He was not self-sustained, but made use of the spiritual resources available to His fellow men.* He worshipped in the home, the synagogue and the Temple; He studied the Scriptures; and above all He lived a life of prayer.

For Him prayer was indispensable, not only as a habit of constant communion in activity (see John 11: 41, 42) but as a practice that involved periods of withdrawal from other occupations. If the actions of others interfered with His plan and privacy, He made opportunity to pray by retiring to some solitary place, even if this meant rising early in the morning or foregoing a night's sleep (for example, Mark 1: 35; 6: 46; Luke 5: 15, 16).

In this life of divine communion, He as man dwelt in the life and the will of God, finding full resources for every need, even those of Gethsemane and the Cross.

3. The act of the Incarnation involved more than a committal to share human experience in a temporary way.

Here was the demonstration in time of Christ's commitment to be *one* with mankind for ever, so that He is both *representative* man and *ideal* man.

(*a*) The Son of God took upon Himself the title ' Son of man ' with such completeness as to become the representative of the whole human race for whom He bound Himself to stand and to act.

Cost Him what it may, their lost condition is His business. Injury done to His brethren is injury done to Him (Acts 9: 4). The neglect of the hungry, naked and deprived is a wound He bears (Matt. 25: 44, 45).

Moreover, this ' Brother ' union with men is an eternal relationship. It does not date from the Incarnation but precedes and explains it. As in Old Testament days it was said of the God of Israel that ' in all their affliction He was afflicted ' (Isa. 63: 9), so the Incarnation is a visible testimony of the continuing oneness of Jesus with men.

(*b*) Further, Jesus was more truly man than any other man for He was without sin—the ideal man.

His manhood was true to the pattern of what God intended man to be. Although He was sent ' in the likeness of sinful flesh ' (Rom. 8: 3) and was ' in all points tempted like as we are ' yet He was ' without sin ' (Heb. 4: 15). He ' knew no sin ' (2 Cor. 5: 21) and ' did no sin ' (1 Pet. 2: 22).

This truth would seem to separate Jesus from men and men from Him but, in the light of the gospel, is seen as a welcome truth for it demonstrates that a sinful condition is not God's intention for men. For in the bond of oneness with men Jesus gave Himself so completely for them and to them that all separation was cancelled and a way made for them to become as He is, which is to become what they were always intended to be. Only thus can they in their turn become ' truly and properly ' men.

Section III.   HIS DIVINE NATURE

1. General evidence to this truth is drawn from:

(a) *the teaching of Jesus Himself;*

(b) *the revelation given by His character and mighty works;*

(c) *the witness of the mighty acts related to His person, such as His Incarnation, Resurrection and Ascension, and the mighty acts done by His followers in His name;* and

(d) *the parts of the New Testament specially devoted to this doctrine,* such as:

> (i) *The Gospel of John,* which reaches its climax in chapter 20: 28, 29, and clearly states its purpose in the two verses which follow:
>
> Many other signs truly did Jesus in the presence of His disciples, which are not written in this book: but these are written, that ye might believe that Jesus is the Christ, the Son of God; and that believing ye might have life through His name.
>
> In this Gospel more than anywhere else in the New Testament is found the *testimony given by Jesus Himself* to His divine relationship with the Father and with the Holy Spirit.
>
> (ii) *The Epistle to the Colossians,* written to show that Jesus is the all-sufficient Saviour (see especially Col. 1: 12–22).
>
> (iii) *The Epistle to the Hebrews,* written to confirm Jewish Christians in the truth that Jesus, the Incarnate Son, more than fulfils the hopes inspired by Old Testament revelation.

2. There are New Testament statements which refer to Jesus as being divine.

At the baptism of Jesus the announcement was made:

Thou art My beloved Son, in whom I am well pleased (Mark 1: 11).

(See also Mark 9: 7; John 1: 1; 5: 23; 10: 30; Acts 20: 28.)

3. To Him are ascribed those powers and perfections which belong only to God:

(a) *Every divine attribute* (John 14: 9; 16: 15; Col. 2: 9).

(b) *The divine holiness* (Heb. 7: 26; Rev. 3: 7).

(c) *The divine love* (John 15: 9; Eph. 3: 19).

(d) *Eternal existence* (John 1: 2; 8: 58; Rev. 1: 11).

(e) *Omnipotence* (Matt. 28: 18; Phil. 3: 21).

(f) *Omnipresence* (Matt. 18: 20; 28: 20).

(g) *Omniscience* (Col. 2: 3).

(h) *Unchangeableness* (Heb. 13: 8).

4. Jesus has performed and will perform works which are possible to God alone.

(a) *Jesus was one with the Father as Creator, Preserver and Governor* (John 1: 3; 1 Cor. 15: 24; Col. 1: 16, 17; Heb. 1: 13).

(b) *He acts as Governor in the moral realm*

(i) *as the giver of law*—' But I say unto you ' (Matt. 5: 28, 32, 34, 39, 44; see also Matt. 7: 24, 26).

(ii) *as Judge* (John 5: 22, Acts 10: 42).

(c) *In the spiritual realm He*

(i) *makes Atonement between God and man* (John 1: 29; 6: 51; Heb. 1: 3).

(ii) *bestows on men its benefits* (Matt. 9: 2; John 11: 25, 26; 17: 2; Acts 2: 33).

5. The Lord Jesus Christ is shown as receiving worship as God.

(a) *By His followers* (John 20: 28; Acts 7: 59, N.E.B. See also John 9: 35–38; Rev. 1: 5, 6).

(b) *By angels* (Heb. 1: 6; Rev. 5: 11, 12).

(c) *By all creation* (Rev. 4: 11).

6. Jesus made claims that can rightly be made only by God.

(a) He claimed to be one with the Father, *to possess divine attributes and to do divine works.* (Note how many of the quotations used in the preceding paragraphs are taken from the words of Jesus Himself.)

(b) He acted as God *by accepting worship* (Luke 24: 52).

(c) Throughout His ministry *His teaching about Himself was presented as a truth to which the Father Himself would testify* (John 5: 36, 37; 7: 16, 17; 8: 18; 12: 27, 28; 15: 26; Matt. 21: 42).

(d) These claims are to be seen in the *light of His character and teaching*.

He who said ' I am meek and lowly of heart ' called for the most searching regard for truth and condemned all forms of self-exaltation.

(e) These claims are to be seen in the *light of Calvary*. They were made at the risk of His life, and eventually earned Him sentence of death (John 5: 18; 10: 33; 19: 7).

(f) These claims are to be seen in the *light of history*. Based on the doctrine that He is the Son of God and the Saviour of men, His Kingdom has grown as He declared it would (Matt. 13: 31–33).

7. The Old Testament witnesses to the doctrine concerning Jesus.

Every advance in divine revelation has an enriching effect on the revelation that preceded it. With the coming of greater light, values not previously perceived are seen to have been there from the first.

This truth is demonstrated in the coming together of the Old and New Testaments. In the hands of Jesus and in the light of the Christian revelation the Old Testament has a glory which it does not display when standing alone.

Of these Scriptures Jesus said, ' they . . . testify of Me ' (John 5: 39) and, in keeping with this claim, the contribution that the Old Testament makes to the Christian message is woven into the text of the New Testament.

The Old Testament supplies more than a collection of texts in support of the gospel message; the doctrine concerning Jesus is shown to be both the climax of its history and the fulfilment of its teaching. This is the particular theme of the Epistle to the Hebrews. (See also Luke 24: 44–47; John 5: 45–47; Acts 2: 16–21, 25–28, 34, 35; 3: 21–26; 8: 30–35; 17: 10–12; 18: 28; 28: 23.)

On occasion this study has been pursued to extreme lengths, and Christian significance has been attributed to Old Testament writings by giving interpretations which are foreign to the meaning conveyed by the words when read in their context. Where such interpretations cannot be shown to have support from the Scripture itself, they have no weight for the purposes of teaching and doctrine.

Section IV. THE UNITY OF THE TWO NATURES IN HIS PERSON

1. The first clause of Article 4 unites and controls the statements already considered in Sections II and III.

(a) In the Lord Jesus Christ the divine and human natures are *united* in *one* Person. There are not two persons, one divine and one human; nor is the Lord Jesus Christ a divided Person, part divine and part human.

(b) This declaration ensures that neither of the two state-ments which follow can be thought of in a way that ignores the other, and certainly not as being in conflict with the other. We do not speak of the deity of Jesus in a way that cancels the teaching that He is truly and properly man, nor of His humanity in a way that cancels the teaching that He is truly and properly God.

2. From time to time within the first four hundred years of Christian history, there arose in the Church teachings about Jesus which denied one or other of the doctrines presented in this Article.

(a) Church Councils were called to deal with the authors and followers of these heretical movements. In some instances deliberation on these matters involved protracted discussion, but they also led to the publishing of carefully worded statements in which orthodox doctrine was set forth in the language of the age.

(b) Concerning the doctrine that Jesus is both God and man, the Church Councils which met at Chalcedon in 451 A.D. declared:

> We all with one accord teach men to acknowledge one and the same Son, our Lord Jesus Christ, at once complete in Godhead and complete in manhood, truly God and truly man, consisting also of a reasonable soul and body; of one substance with the Father as regards His Godhead, and at the same time of one substance with us as regards to His manhood; like us in all respects, apart from sin; as regards His Godhead, begotten of the Father before the ages, but yet as regards His manhood begotten, for us men and for our salvation, of Mary the Virgin. (*Documents of the Christian Church*, Henry Bettenson, p. 73.)

Concerning the doctrine that in His Person the two natures are united, the same Creed contains the teaching that the two natures are

> without confusion, without change, without division, without separation; the distinction of natures being in no way annulled by the union, but rather the characteristics of each nature being

preserved and coming together to form one person and subsistence, not as parted or separated into two persons, but one and the same Son and Only-begotten God the Word, the Lord Jesus Christ.

3. The Incarnation involved for the Son a ministry of self-giving and self-humbling.

He who was rich, for our sakes became poor, humbling or emptying Himself to take the form of a servant (2 Cor. 8: 9; Phil. 2: 7).

4. The purposes of the Incarnation were fulfilled by means of the limitations Jesus accepted.

The self-giving nature of the love of God, and the intensity of the divine purpose to bring men into a living fellowship with Himself could be revealed in no other way.

The might of the divine holiness, love and truth is revealed by the fact that in their strength Jesus won the victory over evil.

Because the Lord Jesus Christ is both God and man, He is

(*a*) *the Supreme Revealer of God* in terms which are effective for all men for all time.

(*b*) *the Brother and Helper of men*, who acts with human sympathy and in divine power (Heb. 4: 15, 16).

(*c*) *the Reconciler, Intercessor and Saviour:*

  (i) uniting the divine and human natures in His person;

 (ii) uniting Himself with all men, and opening the way for the reconciliation of God and man, and man with his neighbour, through His Incarnation and Atonement;

(iii) evoking repentance and faith by His life and death; and

(iv) dwelling in those who receive Him in the power of His risen life.

5. The restriction involved in the Incarnation did not impair the reliability of the teaching Jesus gave.

As the Holy Child He could not manifest the divine attribute of omniscience; instead, He grew in knowledge by the exercise of the mental powers common to men.

The knowledge He gained from the Scriptures and experience was illumined by His constant communion with the Father. He dwelt in the light of God and saw all things in that light. Nothing is properly known until it is known as God knows it and seen as God sees it. This was the nature of the knowledge possessed by Jesus (see John 3: 11–13).

Jesus did not claim to know everything, and said that He could not impart knowledge that belonged to the Father alone and which He did not intend man to have (Mark 13: 32; Acts 1: 7). He did not pronounce on every subject presented by questioners; He distinguished between what was important and unimportant, between the essential and the non-essential (Luke 13: 23–30; John 21: 20–22).

But He knew accurately all that it was necessary for Him to know for His mission of revelation and redemption. He claimed to possess progressive illumination from the Father (John 5: 20) and to know Him in a unique way (Matt. 11: 27; John 6: 46; 10: 15). He knew also from whence He came and whither He would go (John 8: 14), and spoke of the coming work of the Holy Spirit and of His own work as it affected all men for all time.

He claimed to be ' the Truth ', adding that ' heaven and earth shall pass away: but My words shall not pass away ' (Mark 13: 31). He declared that the Father and the Holy Spirit approved His words (Luke 9: 35; John 14: 26; 16: 14) and that men who acted in accordance with His teaching were building on a rock that would withstand every test (Matt. 7: 24, 25).

Section V. HIS NAMES AND TITLES

God . . . hath highly exalted Him, and given Him a name which is above every name: that at the name of Jesus every knee should bow . . . and that every tongue should confess that Jesus Christ is Lord to the glory of God the Father (Phil. 2: 9–11).

1. Each of the names and titles ascribed to the Incarnate Son expresses some aspect of the doctrine concerning Him.

As none of these names or titles is comprehensive enough to stand alone, it is necessary to use some combined form of title such as ' The Lord Jesus Christ ', in which the word ' Lord ' indicates His deity, the name ' Jesus ' His humanity, and the title ' Christ ' His office or mission.

The examples set out below show that every form of title used can be classified in relation to one or more of these three aspects of teaching concerning Jesus.

2. Names and titles which primarily indicate His Deity.

(a) *The Son of God.*

This title declares the position of Jesus within the Trinity. The special right of Jesus to this title is clearly marked in the New Testament where He is called ' the *only* begotten Son ' and ' *the* Son ', and by the references in Rom. 8: 3 and 32 to God sending ' His *own* Son '.

(b) *Lord.*

This title is an acknowledgment of His deity, and of His consequent right to receive the worship and submission of men (Phil. 2: 10, 11).

(c) *The Word.*

This is the somewhat inadequate translation of the Greek term ' *Logos* ', which appears in the original text of John 1: 1, 14 and Rev. 19: 13. Probably the best commentary on its meaning is in Heb. 1: 1–3, where the Son is shown to stand supreme as *the* Word of God in a perfect sense.

These verses present the perfection of

    (i) the *relationship* between Him who speaks and the Word spoken, who is ' the express image of His person ', His Son;

    (ii) the *revelation* this ' Word ' conveys in that He is also ' the brightness of His glory ';

(iii) the *effect* this 'Word' produces upon the whole universe in creating and sustaining power (verses 2 and 3) and upon all mankind in redeeming power (verse 3).

Note also that the 'speaking' activity of this 'Word' involves *all that He is* and *all that He does*, as well as *all that He says*.

3. Names and titles which primarily indicate His humanity.

(a) *Jesus.*

This is His name as man. It is an ordinary Jewish name which He shared with others (Acts 13: 6 and Col. 4: 11). However, the name was specially chosen for it means 'Jehovah is Saviour', thus describing His mission to men (Matt. 1: 21).

Of special interest to Jewish believers was the fact that Jesus is the New Testament form of the Old Testament name Joshua; consequently Jesus was shown as the greater Joshua who leads His people into a better 'rest' than did the Joshua of Old Testament days (Heb. 4: 8–11, N.E.B.).

(b) *The Son of David.*

This was one of the titles given to the expected Messiah (Matt. 21: 9). Jesus being 'made of the seed of David according to the flesh' (Rom. 1: 3), belongs to the Jewish race with all the privileges and promises of Abraham's seed. Being 'of the house and lineage of David' He inherits 'the throne of His father David' (Luke 1: 32; 2: 4) and is the One who fulfils the Old Testament expectations contained in such statements as

Thine house and thy kingdom shall be established for ever before thee (2 Sam. 7: 16; see also Jer. 23: 5, 6; Acts 2: 29–31; 13: 22, 23).

(c) *The Son of man.*

This is a name which could mean simply 'man', thus identifying Jesus with our human condition. It connects Him not only with Israel, but with every 'son of man', even with the least and the lowest who also had 'not where to lay his head' (Matt. 8: 20).

Jesus is also the triumphant Son of man, who will 'come in

the glory of His Father ' (Matt. 16: 27) as Judge, King and Lord
to call all men to account for the way in which they have discharged their responsibility toward their fellows (Matt. 25:
31–34, 37, 44).

4. Names and titles which indicate His office or mission.

(a) The Christ.

This is the Greek translation of the Hebrew title ' The
Messiah ', meaning ' The Anointed One ' (John 1: 41, N.E.B.).
The use of this title gave significance to Peter's words at Pentecost
to the assembled congregation of Jewish people:

> Therefore let all the house of Israel know assuredly, that God
> hath made that same Jesus whom ye have crucified, both Lord and
> Christ (Acts 2: 36).

(b) Saviour (1 John 4: 14; Luke 2: 11).

This title of Saviour is not given to the Son alone, nor is its
use confined to the New Testament.   In the Old and New
Testaments God was known and called upon as Saviour (Isa. 43:
3; Titus 1: 3).

New Testament teaching shows that each Person of the
Trinity is active in the work of salvation:

> But after that the kindness and love of *God our Saviour* toward man
> appeared, not by works of righteousness which we have done, but
> according to His mercy He saved us, by the washing of regeneration,
> and renewing of *the Holy Ghost*; which He shed on us abundantly
> through *Jesus Christ our Saviour* (Titus 3: 4–6).

(c) The Servant of God.

Matthew's reference (12:18) to Isa. 42: 1 identifies the person and work of Jesus with the Old Testament declarations about
the ' Servant ' of God who would fulfil His redemptive purpose
by suffering and death (Isa. 42: 1–4; 49: 1–6; 50: 4–9; 52: 13–53:
12). (See also John 12: 37–41; Acts 8: 32–35; 1 Pet. 2: 22–25.)

The above list is by no means complete but, as with such
other well-known examples as Emmanuel, the Lamb of God, and
the Good Shepherd, the meaning of the title is usually indicated
by the context.

5

THE HOLY SPIRIT

Section I. INTRODUCTION

The person and work of the Holy Spirit are mentioned in Articles 3 and 7, but He is also necessarily concerned with the inspiration of the Scriptures (Article 1), the life and ministry of Jesus (Articles 4 and 6), and the work of saving grace in the lives of men (Articles 7–10).

The doctrine of the Holy Spirit thus includes His *place in the Godhead* as the Third Person of the Trinity, His *work in creation*, His *work as recorded in Scripture*, with specific reference to the life and teaching of Jesus, and His *presence at Pentecost and in the world today*.

Section II. THE HOLY SPIRIT IN THE GODHEAD

1. Article 3 declares that the Holy Spirit is the Third Person in the Godhead, co-equal in power and glory with the Father and the Son.

In the Bible the Holy Spirit is given divine names and titles, is presented as having divine attributes, doing divine works and receiving reverence and worship.

2. The Bible teaches that the Holy Spirit is a Person in the same sense that the Father is a Person and the Son is a Person.

(a) *This truth needs special comment* for in the Hebrew and Greek languages three distinct meanings (breath, wind and spirit) are covered by one word—in the Hebrew *ruach* and in the

Greek *pneuma*. Consequently there are references to movements of the Spirit of God in both Testaments which would seem to indicate that nothing other than a divine force as of a ' wind ' or ' breath ' was at work. But, as the New Testament makes clear, all such actions are the work of One who is a Person as the Father and the Son are Persons.

(*b*) *This was taught most clearly by Jesus Himself.*

In John 14: 16, 17, 26 and 15: 26 Jesus spoke of the Spirit in association with the Father and with Himself, and referred to Him by three names: ' the Comforter ', ' the Spirit of Truth ' and ' the Holy Spirit ', which in themselves are indicative of the Spirit's attributes and mission.

' Comforter ' is an inadequate English translation of the Greek word *Paraklētos*, which is a title given also to the Son (1 John 2: 1), where the English translation is 'Advocate '. The literal meaning of the Greek word is ' One called alongside to help '.

(*c*) *To the Holy Spirit are ascribed all the attributes of personality:*

    (i) *Knowing* (Rom. 8: 27; 1 Cor. 2: 10, 11).

    (ii) *Feeling* (Eph. 4: 30).

    (iii) *Willing* (1 Cor. 12: 11).

    (iv) *All manner of personal action, such as hearing, speaking, guiding, striving, bestowing gifts.*

(*d*) *To disobey the Holy Spirit is to disobey God.*

    (i) Ungodly behaviour by professing Christians 'grieves' the Holy Spirit (Eph. 4: 30).

    (ii) Deliberate deception in spiritual matters is accounted a lie to the Holy Spirit (Acts 5: 3).

    (iii) Words spoken against the Holy Spirit are regarded as blasphemy against a Divine Person (Matt. 12: 31, 32).

3. The Bible teaches that the Holy Spirit is truly God.

(*a*) *Throughout the scriptural record the Spirit of God is regarded as being one with God.*

In the Old Testament all that is implied of the nature of the Lord is also implied of the nature of the Spirit of the Lord.

Words and works spoken of in the Bible as being of the Spirit are also spoken of as being the words and works of God.

The words attributed to ' the voice of the Lord ' in Isa. 6: 8, 9 are quoted in Acts 28: 25 as being the words of the Holy Spirit; in 1 Cor. 3: 16, indwelling by the Spirit is indwelling by God; the Scriptures inspired by the Holy Spirit (2 Pet. 1: 21) are the Scriptures ' given by inspiration of God ' (2 Tim. 3: 16).

(*b*) *The attributes of God are ascribed to the Spirit.*

     (i) *Omnipresence* (Ps. 139: 7).

     (ii) *Omniscience* (1 Cor. 2: 10, 11).

     (iii) *Love* (Rom. 5: 5; Gal. 5: 22).

(*c*) *He is to be reverenced as being divine* (Matt. 28: 19; 2 Cor. 13: 14).

Section III. THE WORK OF THE HOLY SPIRIT

1. Every operation of the Godhead is the work of the Holy Spirit.

He is described in the Nicene Creed as being ' the Lord and Giver of life '. He is the eternal, omnipotent and ever-present Spirit of life and light, working always in the nature of holy love.

2. Two characteristics of the Spirit's work are demonstrated in the Bible.

(*a*) *The manner of His working is both general and selective.*

     (i) *General*. There are operations of the Spirit of God which are of the same nature upon all men, for example, in convicting the sinner of his sin.

(ii) *Selective.* The Spirit of God chooses and equips certain individuals in a particular way for a particular work. All these selective workings, however, are designed to further God's redeeming purpose for all men. One is being used to serve the many.

(*b*) *His work with men has to do with all levels of their being—physical, intellectual, moral, spiritual and social.*

This truth corrects the wrong idea that the Holy Spirit's actions are solely of an extraordinary or miraculous nature.

3. The Holy Spirit was at work in Old Testament days.

(*a*) *He equipped men to fulfil the special duties to which they were called:*

(i) Moses, and those who were called to help him as administrators (Num. 11: 17).

(ii) Bezaleel and his associates in their work of providing worthy material for the tabernacle (Exod. 31: 1–6).

(iii) Gideon and David to be national leaders (Judges 6: 34; 1 Sam. 16: 13).

(*b*) *He inspired the prophets to fulfil all that was involved in their ministry* (Micah 3: 8; 2 Pet. 1: 21, N.E.B.).

(*c*) *The Holy Spirit convicted men generally of their need of righteousness by direct appeal to conscience,* as in Ps. 51: 9–11 and 143: 10.

Encounter with the prophets was encounter with the Holy Spirit (Neh. 9: 30, R.S.V.; see also Heb. 3: 7–11).

(*d*) *In the Old Testament the activity more than the nature of the Spirit is emphasized, but certain prophets declared that a greater manifestation of the Spirit would be given to men.*

The two main expectations were that

(i) the Spirit of God would be fully operative in the Person of the coming Messiah (for example, see Isa. 11: 1, 2; 42: 1; 61: 1);

(ii) in the ' day of the Lord ' the Spirit would be poured out on Israel and upon ' all flesh ' with transforming power (Ezek. 36: 26, 27; Joel 2: 28–32).

4. The Holy Spirit was at work at the Incarnation.

(a) *The message to Mary.*

The angel answered and said unto her, The Holy Ghost shall come upon thee, and the power of the Highest shall overshadow thee: therefore also that holy thing which shall be born of thee shall be called the Son of God (Luke 1: 35).

(b) *At the Jordan.*

Jesus, when He was baptized, went up straightway out of the water: and, lo, the heavens were opened unto Him, and He saw the Spirit of God descending like a dove, and lighting upon Him (Matt. 3: 16).

(c) *In the wilderness.* By the power of the Spirit the tempter was repelled (Matt. 4: 1).

(d) *In testimony to Jesus* as ' the Christ ' or the 'Anointed One ' (see John 3: 34).

(e) *Jesus bore His own witness* to the seal of the Spirit upon Him (Luke 4: 16–21) and to the action of the Spirit through Him (Matt. 12: 28). Finally He joined His own testimony to that of John the Baptist (John 1: 33) concerning Himself as being the One by whom the Spirit would come in transforming power (John 7: 37–39; 15: 26; Acts 2: 33).

Section IV. THE MINISTRY OF THE HOLY SPIRIT

1. The presence and power of the Holy Spirit is indispensable to the work of redemption—a truth The Salvation Army emphasizes with its motto ' Blood and Fire '.

(a) *The greatest blessing that comes from the ascended Lord is the continuing presence of the Holy Spirit with all men in all ages and in all places.*

Jesus taught His disciples that His mission to the world would be continued by the Spirit, and that the presence of the Holy Spirit would make up for any loss they would feel when their Master was no longer with them in the flesh (John 16: 7).

The eternal Spirit of God has always been at work in the world, and the statement that He ' came ' at Pentecost, far from contradicting this truth, means that He who was from the beginning now came upon men in the fulness of His power. It was in this way that the Spirit was ' given ' when Christ ' was glorified ' (John 7: 39).

2. The New Testament represents the Holy Spirit as specially connected with truth, holiness and power.

(a) He is described as ' the Spirit of *truth* (John 14: 17). He makes men see things as they really are. Hence He is sometimes said to be the Revealer (of the truth) and the Witness (to the truth). Thus:

> (i) He enabled apostles and others to understand *the truth* about Jesus and, under His guidance, to record this in the books of the New Testament (John 15: 26, 27; 16: 12, 13).
>
> (ii) He reveals to the sinner *the truth* concerning the great evil of sin, and concerning Jesus as the only Saviour.
>
> (iii) He witnesses, in the hearts of God's people, to *the truth* concerning their salvation and sanctification.

(b) He is ' the *Holy* Spirit. The word ' holy ' reminds us not only of the Spirit's perfect holiness, but also that He is the source of all true goodness or holiness in men. He enlightens the sinner, makes and keeps God's people holy, and produces in them the ' fruit of the Spirit ' (Gal. 5: 22, 23).

(c) He is the giver of *power* for Christian life and service. Jesus told His disciples to wait in Jerusalem until ' endued with *power* '

(Luke 24: 49), and promised that they should ' receive *power*, after that the Holy Ghost is come ' (Acts 1: 8). Paul preached in the ' *power* of the Spirit ' (Rom. 15: 19).

3. The Holy Spirit called into being that fellowship of believers known in the New Testament as ' the Church '.

(*a*) The word ' church ' as used in the New Testament is a translation of the Greek word ' *ekklēsia* ', which means an assembly, or ' that which is called out '. Of itself the word has no religious significance as can be seen by its use in Acts 19: 41. It has, however, a direct association with the word ' congregation ' in the Old Testament when it refers to the ' congregation of Israel ', the people covenanted to God to be ' a kingdom of priests, and an holy nation ' (Exod. 19: 6), and described in Acts 7: 38 as being ' the church in the wilderness ' (that is, at Mount Sinai).

(*b*) In fulfilling His purpose for the world God works not only through individuals but through a chosen community. In Old Testament times the congregation of Israel was this chosen instrument. Today the Christian fellowship has this calling and responsibility. The Church is composed of the people whom God has called together in Jesus Christ, a fellowship which includes all disciples of Jesus irrespective of national and racial backgrounds (Gal. 3: 28; Eph. 2: 14; Col. 3: 11). It is also called ' the Israel of God ' (Gal. 6: 16), inheriting and continuing in the light of the Christian revelation the place and work once given to Israel (see 1 Pet. 2: 9, 10 in relation to Exod. 19: 6 and Hos. 2: 23).

(*c*) The existence of the Church is an act of God, and is a fulfilling in part of His eternal purpose that in the ' fulness of times He might gather together in one all things in Christ ' (Eph. 1: 10).

The Christian Church came into being

> (i) *by the calling and training that Jesus gave His disciples;*

> (ii) *by the Atonement* (Acts 20: 28; Eph. 5: 25); and

(iii) *by the action of the Holy Spirit upon the first company of disciples and upon those who believed in Christ ' through their word '* (John 17: 20; Acts 2: 38, 39, 41, 42, 47).

(*d*) The Church is also described in the New Testament as:

(i) *The flock of which Christ is the shepherd* (John 10: 16).

(ii) *The ' body of Christ '* (Rom. 12: 5; Eph. 4: 15, 16).

(iii) *A temple or building in which the whole is formed of the combined parts.* The ' temple of the living God ', which He indwells by the Spirit, is both the body of the individual Christian (1 Cor. 6: 19) and the one great temple formed of the whole body of the people of God (Eph. 2: 19, 20; see also 1 Pet. 2: 4, 5, and note that this temple includes the people of God of all time).

(iv) *A kingdom which is also a family* (Col. 1: 12, 13; Rom. 8: 14, 17).

(v) *The bride of Christ* (see Eph. 5: 25–32; Rev. 19: 7–9).

(*e*) The Christian fellowship must be seen in the light of the revealed will of God, and not be assessed by its differing structures at any point in its history.

In the figure of the vine and the branches (John 15), the branches are not only joined to the vine but joined with one another through the vine. What is essential to the Church is not a particular form of administration but the living union of its members with Christ and with one another through Christ.

(*f*) The work of the Holy Spirit in relation to the fellowship of believers was

(i) to establish and develop the Christian community and

(ii) to use this Spirit-controlled community as an instrument for the spread of the gospel throughout the world.

Men and women were called to be co-workers with God and were equipped by the Spirit for this twofold ministry. They ' preached the gospel . . . with the Holy Ghost sent down from heaven ' (1 Pet. 1: 12). They confirmed the word ' spoken by the Lord . . . and God also bearing them witness, both with signs and wonders, and with divers miracles, and gifts of the Holy Ghost, according to His own will ' (Heb. 2: 3, 4).

The Holy Spirit, by inspiration and the evidence of events (for example, Acts 8: 1, 26–40; 10: 1–11: 26), guided the onward progress of the early Christian fellowship and delivered its members from the restricting ideas of Jewish exclusiveness (Acts 15: 28, 29).

In fulfilment of Christ's declaration that ' the Holy Ghost . . . shall teach you all things ' (John 14: 26) and ' will guide you into all truth ' (John 16: 12–14), the apostles and their immediate associates produced the books of the New Testament, which serve the ministry of the Church both to itself (' the divine rule of Christian faith and practice ') and to the world.

The Spirit of God also equipped, directed and controlled the early Christians in their missionary service. For example, see Acts 1: 8; 2: 4; 4: 29–31; 13: 2, 4; 16: 6–10.

4. The Holy Spirit still works in the hearts of men in this comprehensive way, dealing both with individuals and with the whole Christian community.

(a) *The Spirit is concerned with relationships: man's relationship with*

> (i) God as Creator and to God in Christ;
>
> (ii) his fellow man; and
>
> (iii) his fellow believers.

(b) *He still calls, appoints and equips believers to serve the Christian fellowship and to be nourished by it.*

This relationship is set forth in

> (i) Rom. 12: 1–8, where ' reasonable service ' is shown to be due both to God and to the Christian community;

    (ii) 1 Cor. 12, where Christians are shown to be dependent upon each other as are the various parts of the body; and

    (iii) Eph. 4: 1–16, where the life and service of the total Christian community is shown as a witness for Christ to the world.

Thus there are gifts of the Spirit which qualify the believer for appointed service (1 Cor. 12), but the prior need is clearly shown in 1 Cor. 12: 31; 13: 1.

(*c*) *He also calls, appoints and equips men to be witnesses for Christ to the world.*

He is willing to use all believers as evangelists, making them ' witnesses to Christ ' and enabling them to share in the ' ministry of reconciliation '.

This ministry combines proclamation and persuasion, supplemented by demonstration of the power of the gospel in the evangelist's own life (1 Tim. 1: 15, 16) and in his relationships with his fellow believers (John 13: 34, 35).

(*d*) *He inspires believers to be concerned about the daily needs of his fellows.*

This is an inescapable requirement of the Christian gospel (Luke 10: 36, 37; 1 John 3: 16–18).

Concern for the souls of men was the bond that brought Salvation Army pioneers together, and concern for human need later gave rise to our varied expressions of social, goodwill, medical and educational service.

A witnessing, caring Movement will continue to fulfil its calling only in so far as it is composed of witnessing, caring people whose hearts are open to the working of that same Holy Spirit who inspired and empowered their fathers.

5. Other New Testament passages which deal with the work of the Holy Spirit are Galatians 5: 16-25 and Romans 8: 1-27.

These passages are concerned with the convicting, converting, transforming work of the Holy Spirit in the human soul. Both speak of Him as the source of the holiness of heart and life made possible by the Atonement.

6. Further teaching about the Holy Spirit is given in Chapters 8, 9 and 10 on the following basis:

(*a*) *All relationships between the Holy Spirit and men are of His initiation.*

(*b*) *His power exceeds all we can ask or think.*

This is true of

    (i) the coming of redeeming life to the soul (John 3: 8);

    (ii) the way in which this life is maintained (Rom. 8: 26; Eph. 3: 20); and

    (iii) the ultimate accomplishment of the work of grace (1 John 3: 2; 1 Cor. 2: 9).

The present ministry of the Spirit in the life of the Christian is spoken of as being an ' earnest ', that is, a pledge or guarantee of a greater manifestation yet to come (Eph. 1: 13, 14; 2 Cor. 5: 4, 5).

(*c*) *The Holy Spirit can be resisted.*

The Spirit of God operates unbidden and often unrecognized in human affairs, but His work of grace in the life of man is not achieved without man's consent. Hence the Scriptures warn that the work of the Spirit can be hindered, His appeals resisted and even refused. There are also commands to ' receive ' the Spirit, to be ' filled with ' the Spirit, and to ' walk in ' the Spirit.

(*d*) *The Spirit works to further the ultimate purposes of God.*

While the decisions of a man can affect the working of the Spirit in his own life, no human action can finally prevent the day when all things shall be summed up in Christ (Eph. 1: 10).

6

MAN'S DISTINCTIVE ENDOWMENTS AND SINFUL STATE

' We believe that our first parents were created in a state of innocency but, by their disobedience, they lost their purity and happiness; and that in consequence of their fall all men have become sinners, totally depraved, and as such are justly exposed to the wrath of God ' (Article 5).

Section I.   INTRODUCTION

The central declaration of this Article is that all men are sinners.

The statement that as sinners men are ' justly exposed to the wrath of God ', presents this truth in relation to God's requirements of man.   Man's sin has separated him from God.

The words ' totally depraved ' present this truth in relation to man himself.   Sinfulness involves moral weakness and depravity.

While the remaining part of the Article refers to man's fallen state as a sinner, it also contains a message of good news.   Sin is revealed as an intruder, an element which was not part of man's original estate.

The statement that man's sinful state is not in harmony with God's purpose for him, prepares the way for the good news that this can be remedied by God's redeeming work in Christ.   If man is subject to the wrath of God, he is also the object of God's redeeming grace.

Section II.   MAN'S DISTINCTIVE ENDOWMENTS

1. Although man is associated with the natural world about him, he is distinct from it.

Physically man is ' of the dust of the ground ', and his earthly life is sustained by the support of the natural order with which he is linked by his physical nature.

In the Scriptures the making of man is represented as the crowning act of God's creative work, which took place in successive stages, rising from the creation of light to that of man. But man is more than a natural being; he does not live by bread alone. His spiritual endowments and the revelation given by the gospel of redemption concerning his place in the divine purpose, invest him with a dignity and value of his own.

These contrasting truths are presented in the first two chapters of Genesis (1: 26, 27; 2: 7) and form a recurring theme in the Bible. The eighth Psalm, with the comment upon it in Heb. 2: 5–11, is an outstanding example:

> When I look at Thy heavens . . . what is man that Thou art mindful of him, and the son of man that Thou dost care for him? Yet Thou hast made him a little less than God, and dost crown him with glory and honour. Thou hast given him dominion over the works of Thy hands (Ps. 8: 3–6, R.S.V.).

2. The endowments which set man apart from the rest of creation are his rational, moral and spiritual powers.

(a) *Man is one being, consisting of body, soul and spirit* (see Article 10).

The body is the material part of man, by which he is related to the natural world around him.

The Bible does not always clearly distinguish between soul and spirit, for the word ' soul ' is used in two ways. Sometimes it includes both soul and spirit, that is, everything other than the physical body (as in Luke 12: 20); at other times as a simple description of individuals (as in Gen. 12: 5). Where distinction *is* made between soul and spirit, *spirit* represents that part of man's nature which can enjoy spiritual fellowship with God, and which can exist apart from the body (as in Eccles. 12: 7; Luke 23: 46; Acts 7: 59), while the word *soul* is used in relation to things of time and sense.

(*b*) *Man has powers of reason* which can rise to the level of reflective, imaginative and abstract thought, and give him power over his environment unknown to the animal creation.

(*c*) *Man has moral powers*. These include a moral *sense*, a moral *urge*, a moral *accountability* and a moral *freedom* (see para. 3).

(*d*) *Man has spiritual and religious powers*—the desire to seek and worship God, and the capacity to respond to the spiritual revelation He gives.

(*e*) *Man has the capacity for progress* and the desire to exert his faculties to this end.

Man has never been given maturity as an initial gift. His capacities develop with use. He rises to his fullest stature when engaged with matters of eternal worth. His deepest satisfactions are found in the right employment of his highest powers (Matt. 16: 26).

(*f*) *Man's natural gifts are impaired by his sinful state* (see sect. VI, para. 2), and suffer further hurt when turned to unworthy ends.

3. Man's moral powers can be seen in the working of his conscience for he is endowed with freedom of choice.

(*a*) *The working of conscience involves moral sense, moral urge and moral accountability*.

The word ' conscience ' means ' a knowledge with ', ' a knowledge that accompanies other knowledge '. According to light received man has a consciousness of moral values; there are actions and attitudes which he judges as being ' good ' or ' bad ', ' right ' or ' wrong ', and experience reinforces the conviction that these considerations ought not to be ignored. Man finds within him an urge to do what he deems to be right and to refrain from what he feels to be wrong. Conscience passes its own judgment upon his conduct, approving when its prompting is heeded and passing condemnation when it is disobeyed (Rom. 2: 14, 15, N.E.B.).

It is true that the moral powers of man are affected by the injury that sin does to all human faculties, but this may not render him completely insensitive to a moral appeal, nor is it an injury that the restoring power of salvation cannot heal. It is to the faulty conscience of men that God speaks, and it is with the imperfect response they give that they take the first steps to restoration.

(b) *Though man has not absolute freedom of action, he has freedom of choice.*

In such matters as birth and the natural laws of existence man has no choice. The restraints imposed by his physical and mental environment may still further reduce the area of his freedom. However, Matt. 5: 41 and Col. 3: 22, 23 speak of the choice retained even within a subject nation or by an enslaved person. Acts done for Christ's sake or for conscience' sake can defy the power of human compulsion. They are the chosen responses of men who refuse to bow to circumstance.

This moral freedom is respected by God Himself, but it exists within His over-ruling government. The gift of freedom of choice will not enable man to evade final judgment. Man can choose to obey or to disobey God's law, but he cannot avoid being held accountable before God for the decisions he makes. (See, for example, in Matt. 23, the freedom of man in verse 37, but his subjection to the judgment of God in verses 38, 33 and context.)

4. Man is not only an individual but a member of a community.

In the divine intention, man is a social being, incapable of achieving his intended development and destiny in isolation. His life is bound up with that of others in terms both of dependence and of obligation to serve. Influences from the past and present affect his life and person, while he in turn can influence the present and future welfare of others. There is a solidarity of the human race by which are shared both benefit and hurt.

God deals with men as individuals, but always as individuals who have a relationship to Himself and to others. The two great commandments on which ' hang all the law and the prophets ' (Matt. 22: 40) are not concerned with man in isolation but in the setting of his divine and human relationships.

Section III.   EVIDENCES OF MAN'S SINFUL STATE

1. Throughout its pages the Bible addresses men as sinners.

(a) *Every man is regarded as a sinner in need of salvation.* The sinfulness of all men is described in the opening chapters of the Epistle to the Romans, culminating in the statement, 'All have sinned, and come short of the glory of God ' (Rom. 3: 23). (See also Isa. 53: 6; 1 John 1: 8, 10.)

(b) *The supreme revelation of the sinfulness of man is given by the teaching, life and death of Jesus.*

By His *teaching* about the guilt that lies in sinful desire apart from its outward expression (Matt. 5: 28), as well as the seriousness of sins of commission (Matt. 18: 6) and omission (Matt. 25: 41–43, 45) against the law of love, Jesus showed how far men fall short of the perfect will of God.

By His *sinless life*, active in holy love, men are confronted with more than a code of laws; in Jesus they meet man as God intended him to be. By comparing their character and conduct with His, men see how much they differ from the divine pattern of manhood.

The death of Christ at the hands of men, for whatever reason they were implicated in this act, is an indictment of man's sinfulness. It also stands as a condemnation of the hurt which the innocent and the helpless suffer at the hands of their fellows throughout all time. The acceptance of the Cross by Him who died ' for our sins ' shows that in the sight of God sin has a significance beyond all human awareness.

(c) *The sinfulness of man is confirmed by human experience.*

The inward witness of conscience will reproach a man when his conduct does not conform to a law of which his mind approves (Rom. 7: 18–24).

The evils manifested in history and found in the arts bear abundant testimony to the moral failure and corruption marking human life, as do the restraints and penalties written into man-made laws for social living.

2. In the Bible man's nature and conduct, as well as the constitution of human society, are shown to be marked by features contrary to the will of God.

(a) *Human sinfulness is not according to God's purpose for man* (Eph. 1: 4; 2: 10).

(b) *It is not according to His act in creating man* (Gen. 1: 26, 31).

(c) *It is not according to the pattern of man given by Jesus.*

Nothing is clearer in the Bible than God's active antagonism to evil and His declared will to overthrow it. This truth is seen most plainly in the atoning work of Christ.

Section IV. THE FALL OF MAN

1. The Bible teaches that sin had its origin in the misuse of the divinest of God's gifts—freedom of moral choice.

The Scriptures speak of Adam and Eve yielding to the temptation of Satan and disobeying the divine command (Gen. 3: 3, 6).

2. For the account of the Fall of man see Genesis 3 and 2: 9, 16, 17, and Romans 5: 12-19.

(a) *Whether the Genesis account is taken literally or as a revelation in parable form of eternal truth, the story of the Fall teaches certain undeniable truths of life and history:*

(i) *All men share a common parentage.* God ' hath made of one blood all nations of men ' (Acts 17: 26), and all equally may receive the blessings belonging to the family of God (Eph. 2: 17–19; Gal. 3: 28).

(ii) *Man is not as he was created.*

(iii) *Man has been exposed and has yielded to temptation from the beginning of history, with unhappy results for himself and his posterity.*

Such truths as these are basic to the whole of scriptural teaching, and nowhere find stronger confirmation than in the life and teaching of Jesus.

(*b*) *The form in which this account is given encourages the readers to look for significant truth beneath the surface.*

The two trees are obviously more than ordinary trees, and the serpent more than an ordinary reptile. This deeper value is all the more apparent when the third chapter of Genesis is read with the Book of the Revelation in which similar language is used. Rev. 12: 9 speaks of the casting down of ' that old serpent, called the Devil, and Satan, which deceiveth the whole world . . . and his angels . . . with him ', and chapter 22: 2 speaks of a great tree of life whose leaves are for the healing of the nations.

For further help see Rom. 5: 12–19, where the redeeming work of Christ is set in the context of the Fall of man. A comparison of Gen. 3 and Matt. 4: 1–11 reveals that the temptations they record are concerned with the same basic principles (see para. 4).

3. The story of the Fall also teaches that the development of man from a state of innocency to a state of spiritual and moral maturity depended upon the right exercise of his freedom of choice.

There is a distinction between these two states of experience. The former, the state of innocency, man had by creation, but the latter could not be realized without his own consent and co-operation.

Maturity in moral and spiritual character cannot be granted as a gift but is gained when, confronted by the choice between good and evil, man freely chooses the good. Thus the loss involved in the Fall included not only the blessings man *already possessed* (innocence and spiritual fellowship with God), but included the loss of what he *might have become* through obedience. His present standing and future destiny were both at stake.

The further truth about the Fall lies in the fact that it was the result of the misuse of man's endowment of freedom of moral choice. The very means by which his destiny could have been realized was the cause of his downfall—a standing illustration of the truth that where there is the greatest potential for good there is also the greatest potential for evil.

4. The temptation presented in the third chapter of Genesis is concerned with basic delusions which have plagued men throughout history:

(a) *That the most desirable state for any man is to be able to do as he pleases, without outward restraint and without accountability.*

It is an astonishing fact that Jesus and Satan sought to persuade men by what appears to be the same appeal—You are to bear the likeness of God (see Matt. 5: 48); ' Ye shall be as gods ' (Gen. 3: 5). There is, however, the widest possible difference between the two interpretations of godliness. On the lips of Jesus the word spoke of holiness and love, but by Satan connoted the untruth that to be godlike meant to have unlimited power for self-pleasing.

(b) *That man can achieve a worthy destiny by acting independently of God.*

The first delusion (see (a) above) directs man to a wrong objective; the second induces him to use a wrong means.

The suggestion that a right and legitimate goal can be reached by a way quicker and easier than God's way appears both in Gen. 3 and in Matt. 4: 1-11; to Eve in relation to her desire for knowledge and to Jesus in relation to the fulfilment of His mission.

(*c*) *That God is unworthy of man's respect and worship* (Gen. 3: 4, 5).

God is here presented as being untrue, as being moved by motives that would deny man his rightful fulfilment.

This defamation of the character of God strikes at the root of a right relationship between man and God, for it would destroy all desire for spiritual fellowship with Him.

Section V. THE NATURE OF SIN

1. Sin is anything that is not in harmony with the will of God.

Article 5, which refers to the sinner's defiled nature (as being ' totally depraved ') and to his wrong relationship with God (as being ' justly exposed to the wrath of God '), speaks also of man being a sinner by inheritance. It is necessary to consider all these aspects of doctrine, together with the principle of sin which lies at the root of man's wrong relationship with God.

Out of the many words used in the Bible to indicate sin none of them is adequate by itself to describe the total ' wrongness ' of the sinner. Hence all brief definitions of sin need the accompaniment of an explanatory comment to show that they are concerned with some aspect of sin rather than with the whole.

Because this wide statement includes faults of which the sinner may not be aware, narrower definitions are required when speaking of conscious and wilful sin.

2. Sin is an offence against God.

It is possible for men to condemn as ' sins ' certain acts or omissions which do not conform to their own standards of judgment, as it is also possible for men to approve that which is an abomination in the sight of God (Luke 16: 15). Instances of this are found in the encounters between Jesus and certain of the Pharisees whom He accused of transgressing the commandment of God for the sake of their tradition, and of teaching as doctrines the commandments of men (Matt. 15: 3, 9).

This definition of sin includes such wrongs as a man may commit against his fellows, or practices which may defile his own person.

These also are sins inasmuch as they are transgressions of God's law, as expressed in the second great Commandment (Matt. 22: 39).

3. God makes known His will for man in more ways than one.

There is the knowledge which comes from *natural* revelation and from *conscience* (Rom. 1: 19, 20; 2: 14, 15). This is deepened by the revelation of the divine nature and will recorded in *the Bible* through the Law, the Prophets and supremely by Jesus, strengthened by the inner testimony of the Holy Spirit in the life of the individual and the Christian community. Beyond the general will of God for all mankind, many are also given a knowledge of His particular will for them as individuals.

4. The light which makes God's law known to man also makes known man's sinfulness to himself.

(*a*) *When confronted by God's requirements a man is made aware that he falls short of God's standard.*

Thus the law serves to bring home to men their need of salvation. The function of the law is to reveal sin, not to cure it, as can be seen in the Epistles to the Romans and to the Galatians (3: 24).

> (i) *It is wrong therefore to regard the keeping of the law as the way of salvation* (Rom. 3: 20).
> (ii) *It is wrong to reject the condemnation God's law brings.*
> So to do is to oppose His saving purpose which, by exposing wrong, makes plain the need of the remedy.

(*b*) *The supreme light comes from Jesus, and none who has knowledge of Him can accept any other standard as God's will for man.*

Thus it can be said that all that is un-Christlike is sin; sin is un-Christlikeness.

The light of Christ's own example either causes the sinner to turn away from Him, loving darkness rather than light or, like Paul, to cry: ' What shall I do, Lord? ' (Acts 22: 10).

(c) *In this light, the root principle of sin is seen to be self-will or self-centredness.* This preference for self-will instead of God's will is repeated in each successive generation. Self takes the place which belongs to God, and selfishness instead of the law of love becomes the rule of life. The outworking of this self-centredness can poison every human relationship and corrupts even such habits as were good in themselves (Matt. 6: 1–5).

This is why everything that is contrary to the will of God can be described as sin. ' Every unrighteousness is sin ' is the literal translation of 1 John 5: 17. This is the outworking of the truth that man is born a sinner, with an inherited disposition to self-pleasing. He himself will not be blamed for this inheritance. His guilt before God will be related to his own conscious wilful actions, and God alone will assess the measure of his personal responsibility for these.

Section VI.   THE EFFECTS OF SIN

1. Sin separates from God.

This is the root injury that sin inflicts upon the sinner.

All other aspects of the damage done by sin to the sinner arise because he is not in a right relationship with God.

Sin is more than the breaking of particular commands; it is inward opposition to the will of God. In so doing the sinner separates himself from God, the source of all true life.

Every life must have some centre, and if the living God does not occupy this central place, then some lesser god will rule. The lordship of self, or of any other god the self chooses to serve, is a turning away from the true God. Ezekiel (14: 7) spoke of ' every one . . . which separateth himself from Me, and setteth up his idols in his heart, and putteth up the stumblingblock of his iniquity before his face '. Jeremiah (2: 13) declared:

> My people have committed two evils; they have forsaken Me
> the fountain of living waters, and hewed them out cisterns, broken
> cisterns, that can hold no water.

There is a real sense in which the sinner cannot remove himself from the love and lordship of the living God. Man is continuously dependent upon God for the very powers he uses against Him. In this misuse of God-derived blessings, the story of the Prodigal Son is the history of mankind. The ' portion of goods that falleth to me ' was taken as a right but was wrongly used, bringing disaster to the lad and grief to the father (Luke 15: 12, 13).

2. Separation from God inevitably brings spiritual loss and consequent depravity.

(a) *It deprives the sinner of those blessings which come solely from fellowship with God.*

Separation from Him who is the source of all goodness cannot but spell the end of personal goodness. To turn aside from the Giver is to forfeit His gifts. When man lacks the protection of divine grace the powers which he possesses are corrupted by sin, the springs of his life are poisoned, his nature becomes totally depraved. This is why sinful conduct is sometimes presented as a revelation of inward wickedness (James 1: 14, 15), and sometimes as a revelation of an inward weakness that is unable to resist temptation which comes from without (2 Tim. 2: 26; Eph. 2: 2, 3).

(b) *The words ' totally depraved ' are not to be taken as teaching that, as sinners, men are completely evil. The depravity of the sinner is total in the sense that every part of his being is affected by the corruption of sin.*

Man is not so possessed by sin that he is incapable of response to good. His reason can be made aware of the folly of yielding to sin and his moral sense can rise in protest against it. Fear of the consequences can also cause him to hesitate before committing wrongdoing, while nobler motives can lead to acts of self-sacrifice.

When Jesus said, ' Ye . . . being evil, know how to give good gifts unto your children ', He recognized that men can respond to good as well as to bad impulses, so that while He did not hesitate to address men as being evil, He also noted the faithfulness with which many discharged their family responsibilities (Luke 11: 11–13).

But man is so possessed by sin that no part of his being can escape its corrupting influence. The whole of the sinner's life is affected because his heart, the very centre of his being out of which come ' the issues of life ', has been corrupted (Prov. 4: 23). This all-inclusive defilement is the inevitable result of the outworking of an inward corruption which manifests itself in all aspects of life (see Mark 7: 20–23).

The *mind* is darkened, especially in its capacity to appreciate spiritual things (1 Cor. 2: 14; Eph. 4: 18; 1 John 2: 11). The *will* is weakened by the pressure of opposing desires. The *moral powers* are impaired. Indulgence in sin can dull the sensitivity of the conscience until it becomes calloused as though ' seared with a hot iron ' (1 Tim. 4: 2), so that a man can ignore or explain away the warnings of the inward monitor.

The taint of pride and self-concern can affect the highest of human endeavours: those of worship and service. Self-approving elements can induce such unworthy attitudes as pride in one's devotion and humility, and self-satisfaction in not being ' as other men are '.

3. Sin brings bondage.

Separation from God leaves man a captive to sin so that ' he is drawn away of his own lust, and enticed ' (Jas. 1: 14; and see Rom. 7: 19).

Every sin committed strengthens sinful habit and brings man more completely under the power of evil from which he is unable to free himself (John 8: 34).

The Bible also declares that sinful man is in bondage to Satan (Acts 26: 18).

4. The sinner, in his separation from God, is in a state of spiritual death.

The Bible speaks of this truth as affecting this life: ' You hath

He quickened who were dead in trespasses and sins ' (Eph. 2: 1). Plainly this does not mean that man is incapable of responding to divine light and grace—but the very opposite (Eph. 5: 14).

The Bible also speaks of a spiritual separation from God which is of a still more serious nature. This is called ' the second death ' (Rev. 21: 8) and indicates a state of eternal separation from God and banishment from His presence (see chap. 11).

5. Because every man's life is bound up with that of the community, the sin of the individual injures others as well as himself.

Those who are ruled by self-interest cannot truly serve their fellows. An ever-growing flood of material and spiritual hurt falls upon the many because of the self-centredness of the few.

6. Left unchecked, sin will increase its hold upon the sinner.

Increased indulgence in sin widens the soul's separation from God. Instead of leading to repentance, the sense of divine condemnation can lead to more open rebellion against the divine will. Indulgence also strengthens the power of sin over the sinner and can multiply the entanglements which confirm him in his sinful ways.

7. The truth about the nature of sin is most fully realized not by its effects on the sinner and on human relationships, but by encounter with the righteousness of God.

(a) *The most serious aspect of the nature of sin is that it is anti-God*, inspiring not only movement away from Him, but hostility toward Him.

This truth is disclosed by man's reaction to Christ and to the Holy Spirit:

> (i) *When challenged by the person of Jesus.* Evil in men's hearts recognized in Him the unswerving foe of wrong and rose up with the desire to destroy Him (John 15: 22–25).

(ii) *When the Spirit of God confronts sin in the human heart* (Gal. 5: 17).

(b) *This truth underlines two important aspects of salvation:*

(i) *The nature of the remedy it brings.*

It is useless to look to God for a salvation that will deal with the consequences of sin, but leave the cause untouched. Still less does He provide a salvation which will cancel the painful consequences of sin but leave undisturbed its doubtful pleasures.

(ii) *The power needed to effect it.*

It is beyond all possibility that man can save himself. He lacks both the power and the will. Nothing but the saving power of God communicated to him by the Holy Spirit, can give him victory over sin.

8. The fact of sin raises questions to which man can give only a partial answer.

This lack is not a disaster, however, for man's salvation does not lie in understanding and explaining, but in experimental committal to the divine power which brings deliverance from the thraldom of sin (Rom. 6: 19–23). When the last, yet still inadequate word about sin has been said, it remains true that ' where sin abounded, grace did much more abound ' (Rom. 5: 20).

Section VII. THE VARIED ASPECTS OF SINFUL-NESS

1. The law of God is concerned with man in all his relationships, with his inner as well as his outer life.

Consequently the Bible speaks of sin in *action, motive, emotion* and *will*.

(a) *In the realm of action,* God's commands are expressed positively (' Thou shalt ') and as prohibitions (' Thou shalt not ').

Hence the divine law can be disobeyed in two main ways:

(i) *by doing those things God prohibits* (sins of commission); and

(ii) *by not doing those things He requires* (sins of omission).

> We have left undone those things which we ought to have done; and we have done those things which we ought not to have done (A general confession from *The Book of Common Prayer*).

(*b*) God's law is concerned also with *men's motives* and is likewise expressed in the same twofold way.

For example, condemnation for acts of dishonesty includes condemnation for the evil of covetousness before the deeds were done, as well as for the sin of the will in deciding to express the desire in action.

On the other hand, not only should good things be done but they should be done for the right reason and in the strength of the right power.

(*c*) Thus the law of God commands and commends certain *attitudes of heart*—such as love to God and man and their expression in action.

Conversely, there is condemnation for cherishing and expressing such emotions as hatred, pride and greed.

(*d*) The divine law is also concerned with *man's will*, desiring that he should cherish the good and give it outward expression, and reject the bad.

Hence, in speaking of the sinful will the Bible laments the absence of good intent:

> The Lord ... in whose ways they would not walk, and whose law they would not obey (Isa. 42: 24, R.S.V.).

and condemns evil intent:

> They ... sold themselves to do evil in the sight of the Lord, provoking Him to anger (2 Kings 17: 17, R.S.V.).

(*e*) To meet the requirements of both the positive and the negative side of God's law, it is necessary to define sin as ' any lack of conformity to, or transgression of, the will of God '. This ' lack of conformity to God's will ' involves the whole person—

action, motive, emotion and will—and a similar interpretation must be given to the word ' transgression '.

For any assessment of guilt in relationship to sin the word ' known ' should be added before ' transgression ' in the above definition (see sect. II, para. 3).

2. In some ways sins of motive, or intent, are to be regarded with greater concern than sins of action.

God sees all actions in the light of the motive that inspires them. ' The Lord looketh on the heart ' (1 Sam. 16: 7). Some acts condemned by men are not so judged by God, for He sees that the doer is free from the wrong motive that men attribute to him (see Mark 14: 4–9). Other acts honoured by men are condemned by God because of the wrong motive they express. Motive is thus the sole sinful aspect of some deeds that outwardly appear to be worthy. Seemingly good actions can be inspired by unworthy motives (Matt. 6: 1–18).

These hidden evils of heart and will are sinful of themselves, whether expressed or not. This truth was specially emphasized by Jesus when He spoke of the guilt of nourishing evil desire in the heart (Matt. 5: 22, 28). The reasons which hold men back from committing some evil deeds may lack all virtue, as when they are restrained by lack of means or opportunity, or by fear of consequences.

3. All sins do not incur equal condemnation.

There are:

(a) *Sins of weakness and sinful bondage*, acts that are not whole-hearted, when the will is set against the deed (Rom. 7: 19, 20).

(b) *Surrender to sudden unexpected temptation*, when no such conduct is premeditated.

(c) *Sins of deliberate intent*, when desire has the full support of the will (Eccles. 8: 11).

(d) *Commitments by which men consciously devote themselves to a life of sinning*, such as a decision to live by the practice of some evil.

(e) *Sins which can be committed only in association with others.*
Hence men lead their fellows to join them in evil practices, often
enticing the innocent (Rom. 1: 29–32).

(f) *Sins of high-handed rebellion against God*, when the sinner
knows what he is doing, and does it by choice and without regret
(Ps. 2: 2, 3).

All guilt is measured by relation to the light the soul has
received, and to the degree in which the whole personality is
involved in the wrongdoing. Thus Jesus said to Pilate: ' He that
delivered Me unto thee hath the greater sin ' (John 19: 11).

4. When a sinner is enlightened by the gospel, more is involved than the question of his sins; he is challenged about his state of sinfulness.

The challenge is important, both for the possibility it provides
and the responsibility it imposes. Here is a cure which will deal
with both the cause and consequences of his sin, and he who is
unwilling to be changed makes his fallen condition his own
choice. To condemnation for his sins is added the condemnation
of rejecting the offer of salvation from them.

Section VIII. THE SINNER 'EXPOSED TO THE WRATH OF GOD'

1. All men are ' exposed to the wrath of God ' (Eph. 2: 3), that is, to the divine detestation of sin.

2. Statements found throughout the Bible concerning the wrath of God should be read in the light of His love and delight in righteousness (Ps. 11: 5–7).

God's wrath against sin is kindled not only because of its
effects, or because of the wilful disobedience of sinners, but
because He abhors its very nature (Ps. 5: 4–6).

The truths that the sinner is exposed to the wrath of God, but that he is also the object of His love, are not at variance. God's love for men does not cancel His hatred of their sin, neither does all the sin of the world cancel His love for the sinner. His love is a holy love which is completely antagonistic to sin, but which is expressed in seeking to separate man from his sin and to produce in him this same attitude of hatred toward it.

3. God acts with forbearance toward the sinner.

Although sinful man is *exposed* to the wrath of God (Rom. 2: 5) he *is not subject to the full expression* of God's displeasure (Ps. 103: 10, R.S.V.; Ps. 130: 3; Nahum 1: 6; Isa. 48: 9).

(*a*) *This is a restraint of grace*, proclaimed in all passages of the Bible which refer to the forbearance, the longsuffering and the mercy which God shows to all mankind.

(*b*) This forbearance is:

    (i) *open to abuse* (Rom. 2: 4, 5);

    (ii) *open to misinterpretation*.

The immunity from judgment which sinners appear to enjoy (Job 21: 7–15) does not mean that there is divine indifference to sin, or weakness of divine government, or that declarations of impending judgment are false alarms (see Rom. 2: 2–9). The explanation is that ' the Lord is not slack concerning His promise, as some men count slackness; but is longsuffering to us-ward, not willing that any should perish, but that all should come to repentance ' (2 Pet. 3: 9).

4. Yet divine mercy does not mean the abandonment of divine judgment.

The Bible contains many references to the warnings of God's impending judgments, given with the purpose of bringing men to repentance.

Jesus taught that what had befallen those singled out for special judgment, as that which came upon the people of Sodom (Gen. 18: 32), was not final judgment. They, with all other men, still await God's final verdict (see Matt. 10: 15; 11: 20–24).

He also corrected those who taught that all disasters were instances of divine displeasure, but repeatedly warned them of the judgment that would fall on Jerusalem and on a people who continued to neglect the day of their visitation (see Luke 13: 1–9, 34, 35; John 9: 1–3).

Psalm 106 shows how the dealings of God with Israel were marked by acts of judgment and of mercy, thereby providing a summary of one of the great themes of the Old Testament prophets (see also Heb. 12: 5–11; Rev. 3: 19).

5. The sinner is 'justly exposed to the wrath of God' for the sin in his life for which he is personally blameworthy, not for his sinful state by inheritance (Ezek. 18: 20).

The sinner is answerable for his own misdeeds and for the hurt these may have caused to others. The suffering which men endure because of the sins of others is not a sign of divine displeasure. God's wrath is directed against those who are responsible for the injury (Matt. 18: 7).

Section IX. WORDS USED IN THE BIBLE TO DESCRIBE SIN

In addition to the words used to identify particular sins (murder, adultery, deceit, envy, pride, etc.), a number of terms are used which describe aspects of sinfulness in a collective way.

1. The three words used most frequently in the Old Testament appear together in Exod. 34: 7, where we read of God forgiving iniquity, transgression and sin.

These words have equal prominence in the New Testament where they appear as translations of Greek words which are closely related to parallel Hebrew expressions in the Old Testament.

(a) *Iniquity* means something which is twisted or perverted, and thus indicates the spoiling, depraving aspect of sin.

(b) *Transgression* conveys the idea of rebellion. It is linked with the word *trespass*. Both carry the meaning of 'going beyond' or 'stepping aside from' a commandment. Here sin is presented as disobedience to God's law.

(c) *Sin*, as used in this text, is intended to convey a meaning distinct from that covered by iniquity or transgression. The distinctive meaning of the Hebrew word translated as 'sin' is 'failure to meet a requirement, or a standard', 'missing the mark', 'coming short'. This is also the meaning of the Greek term translated by the word 'sin' in the New Testament, as in Rom. 3: 23, 'For all have sinned and *come short* of the glory of God'. Thus the word 'sin' when used in its precise sense draws attention to the failure and weakness associated with the fallen condition of man.

The phrase, ' to do *evil* in the sight of the Lord ', and the word ' *wickedness* ' are, generally speaking, translations of original words meaning that which is *bad, morally wrong*, or the *opposite of all good*.

Sin is also presented as being the opposite of good by the use of the words, ' *ungodliness* ', ' *unrighteousness* ' and ' *lawlessness* '. There are other words used to describe sin, but the overall ideas conveyed can be grouped:

(i) In relation to God's government, sin is disobedience, rebellion, lawlessness, transgression and iniquity.

(ii) In relation to God's nature, sin is ungodliness, un-holiness, self-centredness and defilement.

2. The three words 'flesh', 'world' and 'self' do not necessarily have a sinful connotation; the meaning intended is determined by the context in which they appear.

(a) *The flesh*. This word is used in the Bible in at least three distinctive ways, as referring to:

(i) *the physical body* (2 Kings 4: 34; Luke 24: 39);

(ii) *all mankind* (Gen. 6: 13; Isa. 40: 5; Joel 2: 28), very often in the sense that indicates the mortal limitation and the frailty of humanity (Isa. 40: 6; 1 Cor. 15: 50); and

(iii) *human nature when infected and corrupted by sin* (Gal. 5: 17; Eph. 2: 3; 2 Peter 2: 10).

The Bible nowhere teaches that bodily functions are of themselves evil or that sin has its seat in man's physical nature. The perversions and corruptions of natural appetites and instincts mentioned in Gal. 5: 19–21 are a result and not a cause; they are but the revelation of an inward *spiritual* disorder. When these same faculties are sanctified by the Holy Spirit, their expression is characterized by ' goodness ' and ' temperance ' (self-control) (verses 22, 23).

Declarations about the evil nature of the ' flesh ' are condemnation of the evil power that corrupts human life. They do not refer to the body itself, which can and should be presented ' a living sacrifice, holy, acceptable unto God ' (Rom. 12: 1).

Thus in place of the word ' flesh ', other English translations use such language as the ' lower nature ', ' sinful nature ' or the ' corrupt nature ', while in doctrine this corrupting power is often spoken of as ' inbred sin '.

To live ' according to the flesh ' means to live according to the manner of life which yields to sin and is corrupted by it, while to live ' according to the Spirit ', means to live a life yielded to and sanctified by the Spirit of God (Rom. 8: 5).

(*b*) *The world*. This word can mean:

(i) *The created world*, as in Eph. 1: 4, ' before the foundation of the world '.

(ii) *The race of mankind*, as in John 3: 16, 17, 19.

(iii) *This world of time* as contrasted with the ' other world ' (John 12: 25). Here the temporary nature of this world is presented (1 Cor. 7: 31). In many instances where the Authorized Version gives ' this world ', the Greek text has ' this age ' or ' this life '.

(iv) *The system which man has built up in his state of spiritual separation from God.* It is in this fourth sense that the word has evil implications. The ' world ' is used with this meaning chiefly in the Fourth Gospel and in the First Epistle of John.

The worldly spirit leaves God out of its reckoning; its values are those of time, of ' this age ' and of material things. Its motives are marked by selfishness, greed, expediency and aggression, characterized in 1 John 2: 15, 16 as being dominated by ' the lust of the flesh, and the lust of the eyes, and the pride of life '.

In this sense it is anti-Christ, resenting the Saviour's condemnation of its condition and principles (for example John 7: 7; 8: 23; 15: 18, 19). The power of this resentment was revealed by its share in the crucifying of Jesus, an exposure of its nature all the more revealing in that the people in whom this spirit was expressed were religious leaders.

Separation from the spirit of the world does not involve loss of contact with and influence upon men. The manifestation of another way of life, which has a different Lord and is possessed by another Spirit, is the very means by which the world will be converted (John 17: 15, 18, 20, 21).

(c) *Self.* Primarily, self means a person's own individuality, and in this connection is used in an innocent and unoffending sense. The law of God allows man to love himself, provided that this love is in harmony with the rest of the great commandments. The wrong lies in a love for self which takes the place of love for God and for others.

The sinful aspect of this word is set forth in sect. V, para. 4 (c). This is the self-centredness which rules the life in opposition to God and His will.

It will thus be seen that these three words have a sinful meaning only when they are being used to express a state of separation from God.

7

SALVATION PROVIDED

'We believe that the Lord Jesus Christ has, by His suffering and death, made an atonement for the whole world, so that whosoever will may be saved' (Article 6).

Section I. INTRODUCTION

1. Three main doctrines are presented by this Article of Faith:

(a) *The death of the Lord Jesus Christ was an atoning death.*

(b) *His atonement provides the possibility of salvation for all mankind.*

(c) *The acceptance of salvation requires a decision which each man must make for himself; he must be willing to be saved.*

As Articles 7–10 deal with what it means to be saved, this chapter is limited to consideration of the saving atonement Christ has made for all men, and to any other kindred matters not included in the following chapters.

At the same time, Article 6 is linked with the two previous, as well as the three following Articles, for each makes its own contribution to the doctrine of God as Redeemer.

2. The doctrine of Christ as Saviour covers a wide range of teaching.

Consequently, a number of descriptive words are used though none is adequate by itself to describe the whole doctrine.

In this Article of Faith the word ' atonement ' is used but, strictly speaking, atonement expresses only one aspect of the truth. Its exact contribution is to declare that by the work of Christ as Saviour the estranged sinner is made ' at one ' with God. It thus refers to the change of relationship produced by this work of grace, but as Christ as Saviour does more than provide a change of relationship with God other words are needed.

In a general setting the word ' atonement ' is employed in a representative way to describe the whole of the doctrine, but in this chapter ' atonement ' will be used in its exact meaning and, where necessary, the word ' redemption ' will be used to describe the total saving work of God in Christ.

It is also necessary to add that as man has no separate vocabulary for the spiritual life, all the specialized words used to present the doctrine of redemption prove in some way or other to be inadequate.

3. Redemption is God's supreme work.

(a) *It is divine in conception and supreme in execution.* Man has no power to conceive it and no power to effect it.

Whereas other divine works are described as being effected by the utterance of the word of God (as in Ps. 33: 9), this work involved a personal encounter in Christ with human suffering, sin and death. The resurrection reveals the ' strength and the might . . . exerted in Christ ' to raise Him from the dead (Eph. 1 : 20, N.E.B.).

(b) *It is therefore a unique work,* standing alone as a ' once for all ' action for which all the rest of human experience can provide no adequate means of comparison.

(c) *Because it is a supreme work it communicates supreme blessings,* and opens to man the possibility of a relationship with God impossible of realization by other means.

(d) *It is likewise a matter of supreme importance to all mankind.* Declaration of this doctrine is the central message of the Scriptures and the chief duty of the believer.

4. Man is dependent upon God not only for His saving action, but also for revelation concerning it.

Hence the Christian gospel gives equal emphasis to:

(*a*) *the historical fact that Jesus died on Calvary* and

(*b*) *the eternal significance which this event has for men.*

Old and New Testaments contribute to this revelation. What is said in the New Testament is anticipated and illustrated by the Old, and the revelation given by the Old Testament is fulfilled and interpreted in the New.

5. Every statement about the redeeming work of God must be seen in relation to the overall truth.

This provides a safeguard against the error of taking one aspect of the truth as the whole truth.

(*a*) Although it is rightly said that the Lord Jesus Christ made an atonement for the sins of the world, this doctrine must never be presented in a way which contradicts the doctrine of the Trinity. Father, Son and Holy Spirit are undivided in essence, and are involved in every divine work—see 2 Cor. 5: 19: ' God was in Christ, reconciling the world unto Himself, not imputing their trespasses unto them.' Thus it is correct to speak of redemption as being the work of *God*, and also as being the work of *Christ*.

(*b*) Nor does the suffering and death of Jesus stand apart from the rest of His mission. The Incarnation, Crucifixion, Resurrection and Ascension are all part of the divine work of redemption.

The Incarnation was necessary to redemption (1 Tim. 1: 15; Heb. 2: 17).

The Crucifixion, Resurrection and Ascension are also necessary to one another as aspects of the one redeeming work. He ' who was put to death for our trespasses ', was ' raised for our justification ', and now appears ' in the presence of God on our behalf', ' able for all time to save those who draw near to God through Him, since He always lives to make intercession for them ' (Rom. 4: 25; Heb. 9: 24; 7: 25, R.S.V.).

(c) The words 'suffering and death' imply more than *physical* suffering. This suffering unto death no man can fully understand. The nature of this hidden agony is indicated by the inner experience of Jesus in Gethsemane (Matt. 26: 37, 38; Luke 22: 44) and by similar experiences (for example, John 12: 27; Mark 15: 34).

(d) The use of the past tense in the words ' has . . . made an atonement ' marks the end of a chapter, but not the end of the message concerning God's activity in redemption.

The past tense, ' has made ', presents the triumphant aspect of Calvary, also spoken of as the finished work of Christ (John 19: 30; Rom. 6: 10; Heb. 10: 12).

But as Article 6 shows, it is a work that was done in preparation for a subsequent work—' so that whosoever will may be saved '. He, who as Saviour had accomplished a work *for* men, willed to do a work *in* them and *through* them. His self-giving in becoming man and dying for men prepared the way for a further giving from the throne of His ascended glory (John 7: 39; Acts 2: 33; Eph. 4: 8) and the final consummation of the Kingdom (Acts 3: 21; 1 Cor. 15: 24, 25).

(e) The words ' has . . . made an atonement ' must never be taken to indicate that the work Christ has done can be viewed in detachment from Him. No man can say that he will benefit by His atoning work, yet have no dealings with Him who effected it.

Men are not saved by believing a doctrine, nor are they saved by the cross of wood upon which Christ suffered. Salvation comes through Him who suffered there and ever lives to save. He redeems men by identifying Himself with them, and men receive the blessings of His redemption by identifying themselves with Him (see chap. 8 ' Salvation Received '). For all men He is both the way to the Father and the means by which the fulness of God's saving grace can come to them (1 John 5: 12).

(f) The words ' for the whole world ' refer, as in 1 John 2: 2, to the world of mankind, but the New Testament speaks also of the reconciling work of Christ having an even wider application (Rom. 8: 21, 22, R.S.V.; Eph. 1: 9, 10; Col. 1: 19, 20).

(g) Finally, the work of redemption is not the only purpose served by the suffering and death of the Lord Jesus Christ. By His suffering and death

> (i) He crowns and completes His revelation of the divine nature (1 John 3: 16);
>
> (ii) He makes a supreme appeal to men, drawing forth the love and trust of those for whom He died (1 John 4: 19) and
>
> (iii) He establishes His lordship in every realm (Rom. 14: 9; Phil. 2: 9, 10).

Section II. THE ATONING DEATH OF JESUS

1. The death of Jesus at the hands of men was an essential part of His mission.

(a) *Salvation through Christ was eternally ordained* (1 Pet. 1: 18–20).

(b) *Because His death was eternally ordained, it was prophetically proclaimed* (Acts 3: 18; 1 Cor. 15: 3).

(c) *Although in one aspect the Crucifixion was the work of men, they were acting by God's permissive will* (Acts 2: 23).

(d) *The Crucifixion was also dependent upon the obedience of Jesus.*

As well as being given by the Father (as in John 3: 16; Rom. 8: 32), Jesus gave Himself. He was ' obedient unto death, even the death of the cross ' (Phil. 2: 8). The Lord Jesus Christ was not the victim of circumstances over which He had no control. He could not have been crucified without His own consent (John 10: 11, 17, 18).

(e) *The death of Jesus was followed by His Resurrection and Ascension, and by the outpouring of the Holy Spirit.*

This is evidence that His redeeming mission was fulfilled, and is the divine testimony to the completion of His work (Rom. 6: 10; Acts 2: 32–36).

2. Jesus died as the Saviour of mankind.

(a) *There is a wide difference between the meaning Calvary had for Jesus and that which it had for the majority of those who witnessed His Crucifixion.*

His accusers accounted Him a blasphemer, a disturber of the peace, and a threat to the stability of the nation (Mark 14: 64; Luke 23: 2; John 11: 47–50; 19: 7). In their eyes His Crucifixion was the means by which His life and influence would be ended. To Him His death would be the means by which His mission would be eternally fulfilled (John 12: 24).

No one or nothing could prevent Jesus from giving His death the meaning He chose. Thus while yielding His body into the hands of men for the accomplishing of *their* will, He was also committing His body, soul and spirit to the Father for the accomplishing of *His* will.

(b) *The Scriptures also show that Calvary had an eternal significance.*

Concerning this mystery the Bible declares that Jesus was laying down His life for us (1 John 3: 16), suffering for sins, the just for the unjust (1 Pet. 3: 18), bearing our sins in His own body on the tree (1 Pet. 2: 24). His Blood was being shed for many for the remission of sins (Matt. 26: 28). He was dying for the ungodly (Rom. 5: 6), offering one sacrifice for sins for ever (Heb. 10: 12). He who knew no sin was being made sin for us (2 Cor. 5: 21), ' being made a curse for us ' to redeem men from the curse of the broken law (Gal. 3: 13).

(c) *The death of Jesus is the climax of His work as the Son of man.*

He accepted the Cross for man's sake, as a shepherd who seeks the lost until he finds it. By the Incarnation He had identified Himself with man in his human condition; on Calvary He gave Himself for men as the Sin-Bearer.

(d) *The death of Jesus is also the climax of His mission on earth as the incarnate Son of God* (Phil. 2: 8).

Standing equally with the truth that in His death and its eternal implications (as the great High Priest and Intercessor) He represented *men to the Father*, is the truth that in all aspects of

His earthly ministry (as the great Revealer) He represented *God to man* (John 1: 18; 14: 8, 9).

Thus He fully expressed the divine nature. The work of Christ is the work of God. Calvary does not mark any change in the attitude of God to man, but *reveals* what this attitude has eternally been and *provides* the means by which it was fully expressed. The sacrifice made by the Son was in no way the cause of God's love for the sinner; it was the *outcome* and the *manifestation* of that love (John 3: 16; 1 John 4: 9, 10; Rom. 3: 25; 2 Cor. 5: 19). That is to say, Calvary is of eternal significance. The Cross is a fact of eternity as well as a date in human history (Rev. 5: 6; 1 Pet. 1: 18-20).

(*e*) *The heart of the gospel lies in the truth that Jesus gave Himself both as Son of God and as Son of man.*

In the Incarnation the eternal Son of God gave Himself as the Son of man, and Calvary marked the consummation of His committal. He gave and ever gives Himself both as the Son of God (Gal. 2: 20) and as the Son of man (John 3: 14). While shrinking from none of the implications of His identification with man (as in Heb. 2: 14-18), He retained His oneness with the divine nature, resolving in His own Person everything demanded by this work of grace.

Thus in Himself He is the Reconciliation and the Reconciler; the Way by which sinful man can find restoring grace and the Channel through which redeeming blessings flow.

(*f*) *The Crucifixion is seen also as an act of man. Jesus died not only for men, but by the hands of men.*

This is a revelation of the inclination of the human heart to reject the light which exposes its sin. Part of the work of Jesus was to show men what they ought to be, but His call for personal and social righteousness was rejected by those who, by planning His death, sought to silence Him once for all. This is ever the spirit of the world (John 7: 7).

Jesus could not prevent men rejecting Him. Coercion was not one of His weapons. God always deals with men as free agents and, as such, men crucified Jesus because they preferred darkness to light.

This pattern of rejection belongs to all ages (Matt. 5: 10–12; Acts 7: 51, 52). Those who brought Jesus to His death were not sinners above all men. They were, in the main, responsible leaders who saw their ways branded by Jesus as wrong—a truth they could not bring themselves to admit.

Thus while the Cross stands as a sign of God's will to save men, it also stands as a symbol of man's opposition to the disturbing Lordship of Christ. Each man must decide for himself what the Cross is to mean to him.

3. The Cross is the place of victory as well as the place of suffering.

The crucified Christ is to be seen, not only as a suffering victim, but as the victorious challenger of the power of evil.

(a) *Calvary marked a crucial point in Christ's contest with evil.*

Throughout His earthly life Jesus had consistently denounced evil and victoriously resisted its attacks upon Himself. He who ' was in all points tempted like as we are, yet without sin ' (Heb. 4: 15) could say as He approached the Cross, ' The ruler of this world is coming. He has no power over Me ' (John 14: 30, R.S.V.). Acting, not as Deity from the throne of omnipotence, but as the Son of man in the moral force of holy love, Jesus faced the final challenge.

(b) *The New Testament reveals the Cross as the place where evil suffered its decisive defeat.*

Christ bore the sin of men, not to be crushed by it, but to bear it away. He was acting as the strong Deliverer releasing the captive (Luke 11: 20–22). The issue of this encounter was the Resurrection. Christ came forth as Conqueror in the power of His once-for-all victory (Heb. 10: 12–14, R.S.V.; Rom. 6: 9, 10; Col. 2: 15).

(c) *His identification with men, which meant that He suffered for them, means that they can share in the triumph He won for them* (Rom. 6: 6; see also Rom. 8: 3; 2 Cor. 5: 14, 15).

(*d*) *The crucified Christ is the conqueror of the very forces that seemed to be conquering Him.*

Trusting Himself to the Father's hands, Jesus yielded His body to the worst that evil could do, but by this means He

> (i) revealed the impotence of evil to hurt those who do not yield to its power;
>
> (ii) demonstrated the power of divine love over the worst that the enmity of sinful man can do; and
>
> (iii) transformed the Cross from a symbol of shame into the sign of man's salvation.

Section III. THE NATURE OF SALVATION

1. The distinctive words used to describe the gospel of redemption are now considered.

(*a*) The word 'atonement' appears frequently in the Authorized Version of the Old Testament, where it is a translation of the Hebrew word meaning 'to cover' or 'to wipe away'. Thus the Day of Atonement was given to restore a sense of fellowship between God and the nation (Lev. 16), and personal sacrifice to do the same for the individual (Lev. 1 : 4).

The word 'atonement' appears only once in the Authorized Version of the New Testament (Rom. 5: 11). In many translations it does not appear at all, for the Greek here translated 'atonement' is elsewhere translated 'reconciliation', as in Rom. 5: 10.

Thus 'atonement' and 'reconciliation' are equivalent words. They signify the act of making 'at-one', of bringing together in friendly relationship those who formerly were at variance. The Hebrew word is also translated 'Mercy Seat' (Exod. 25: 17).

(*b*) The words 'redeem', 'redemption' and 'ransom' are closely associated (see Rev. 5: 9; Eph. 1 : 7; 1 Tim. 2: 6).

These words present the idea of deliverance being given to one in helpless bondage, as the deliverance of Israel in Egypt, or the freeing of a slave or a condemned prisoner.

References to Christ acting as a ransom (Matt. 20: 28; Mark 10: 45) draw attention to the truth that this liberation was effected by God alone and at great cost. Men were ' not redeemed with . . . silver and gold . . . but with the precious blood of Christ ' (1 Pet. 1: 18, 19).

The use of these words in the Scriptures is associated also with the idea of the *claim* redemption makes upon the redeemed:

> Know ye not that . . . ye are not your own? For ye are bought with a price (1 Cor. 6: 19, 20).

(*c*) The Greek word translated ' propitiation ' in the Authorized Version and ' expiation ' in the Revised Standard Version, appears in Rom. 3: 25, and 1 John 2: 2; 4: 10, and presents the truth that the saving work of God in Christ provides forgiveness for men justly exposed to His wrath.

The form of the word used in Rom. 3: 25 can be translated: ' Whom God hath set forth to be a *mercy seat* through faith in His Blood.'

Associated with this aspect of doctrine are references to ' remission of sins ' and to ' justification by faith ' (see chapter 8).

(*d*) The words defined above show that the salvation of Christ cancels the *separation*, the *bondage* and the *condemnation* brought by sin, and in this sense they are detailed applications of the truth that ' where sin abounded, grace did much more abound ' (Rom. 5: 20).

Thus, in varied forms the work of salvation is compared to the recovery of the lost, the redeeming of a slave, the reconciling of an enemy, a resurrection from the dead, the deliverance of a captive, the justifying of one rightly condemned, the cleansing of the defiled, and adoption into a family and a kingdom.

(*e*) The form of this teaching directs attention to the means by which these benefits come, pointing to the Cross and speaking of reconciliation, redemption, propitiation, justification, cleansing through Christ's Blood and life through His death.

This aspect of the gospel is supported by those figures of speech which present Christ as the Saviour, the Lamb of God, the Good Shepherd, the Way to God, the High Priest offering sacrifice for sin; the Advocate, Intercessor, Mediator and Ransom; and the Inaugurator of the New Covenant.

Nowhere does an illustration or allegory exactly correspond in every detail. Hence no figure of speech should be carried further than is warranted by the context and fidelity to basic doctrine.

2. The wideness of the purpose of redemption is clearly revealed by Bible statements about Christ giving Himself as a sacrifice for the sins of mankind.

The Lord Jesus Christ died in order that:

(i) *Sinners can be forgiven for His sake* (Eph. 1: 7; 4: 32; Col. 1: 14; 1 John 2: 12).

(ii) *Man can be separated from his sin* (Gal. 1: 4; Heb. 9: 26; 1 John 3: 5).

(iii) *The works of the devil can be brought to naught, and his power over men broken* (Heb. 2: 14; 1 John 3: 8).

(iv) *Man can be drawn to Christ and thus reunited with God* (John 12: 32; 2 Cor. 5: 19).

(v) *Man can become a partaker of the divine life* (John 3: 16; Gal. 4: 5; 1 Pet. 2: 24).

(vi) *Christ can become the Lord of men's lives, and His life their example* (2 Cor. 5: 15; 1 Pet. 2: 21; Phil. 2: 5).

(vii) *The corporate life of men can be transformed.*
Those who come into this new relationship with God come also into a new relationship with one another. This is the fellowship of redeemed believers who are consecrated by the death of Christ to be witnesses to His grace (Eph. 2: 15, 16; 5: 25–27; 1 Pet. 2: 9).

Redemption's dominating purpose, which unites the various ways in which it is expressed, is the transformation of sinful man into the divine likeness.

This transformation is effected by the Holy Spirit who works in men in the power of Christ's risen life, to put an end to their bondage to sin and to communicate the divine nature.

3. In the New Testament references are made to the Blood of Jesus Christ as well as to His death or to His Cross.

Although in John 19: 34 we read of the Blood of Jesus being shed on Calvary in a physical sense, nearly all New Testament references are symbolic, signifying the saving power released by His death. Jesus Himself used this form of speech (see Matt. 26: 28; John 6: 53).

This has to be understood against the background of the Old Testament. ‾ne Jews were taught to regard blood with special reverence. To them it represented the life of an animal or of a man. Animal blood was never used for any purpose other than for making sacrifice to God. All blood not thus used was poured on the ground.

> The life of the flesh is in the blood: and I have given it to you upon the altar to make an atonement for your souls: for it is the blood that makes atonement for the soul. Therefore I said unto the children of Israel, No soul of you shall eat blood (Lev. 17: 11, 12).

In keeping with this Old Testament way of thinking, New Testament references to the Blood of Christ must be understood to refer to the life of Jesus in its total value—the life He lived, the death He died and His risen and ascended glory.

It is with His Blood, that is, with all the value of His triumphant life and death, that He entered heaven (Heb. 9: 12). In this same manner, in the power of an endless life, He enters the heart of man, the fulfilling of John 6: 53–57. So that ' being saved by the Blood ' means being saved by the power of the life, the death and the rising again of the Lord Jesus Christ.

Section IV. EXPLANATIONS OF THE WORK OF REDEMPTION

1. The history of Christian teaching has been marked by various attempts to explain the work of redemption.

That is to say, efforts have been made to answer the question: Why is there redemptive value in the death of Jesus?

Each of the following answers presents an aspect of the truth, but none provides more than a partial explanation.

(a) *His death as a ransom* speaks of a price paid on man's behalf by which he is freed from an obligation he is unable to meet himself. Here emphasis is placed on the teaching that Christ is a Substitute for men—One who stands for them and meets obligations on their behalf.

(b) *His death satisfies the demands of the divine law.* On the Cross Jesus made and presented, on behalf of sinners, a sacrifice of such infinite value that makes it possible for God to allo⋯ His love and mercy to flow in forgiveness to those who repent and trust the Saviour. At the same time God maintains His justice, upholding His law and showing to all the terrible evil of sin.

(c) *His death is the victory over evil which frees men from its bondage.*

(d) *His death makes the strongest possible appeal to the conscience and the affections of man,* convincing him of God's love and evoking repentance.

Each of the above has value, yet if substitution is given as a complete explanation, there is the danger that the need for man to be identified with Christ might be overlooked.

Similarly, if ransom or satisfaction are accepted as complete answers, they could obscure the sanctifying purpose in salvation.

No explanation of the saving work of God in Christ is adequate that does not include the full scope of redemption outlined in sect. III, para. 2.

2. However helpful such explanations may be they are not essential to salvation.

The fact that Christ is Saviour, the full and final revelation of God's will and nature, is greater than any explanation of the fact.

(*a*) The Cross directs its challenge to the *lives* of men, to their guilt and failure. This is the primary challenge of the gospel. It is possible for a man to be able to give an impressive exposition of the doctrine of redemption, yet fail to have any personal knowledge of its life-changing power. It is true also that many who accept Christ as Saviour are unable to express the redeeming value of the Cross save in a word of simple testimony.

The experience of salvation is available to all believing souls, independent of their ability to explain the manner of its operation; indeed, this they will never be fully able to do (1 Tim. 3: 16; Rom. 11: 33, 34; John 3: 8). Their confidence rests on Christ— on what God has done and is now doing through Him.

(*b*) Finally, the meaning of redemption shines in the light of Christ's own life and death. He is His own interpreter. It is in the light of the manger and the Cross that men have the clearest revelation of the love of God, the magnitude of sin, the costliness of redemption and the importance of salvation.

Section V.   THE EXTENT OF GOD'S SAVING PURPOSE

The Bible makes it clear that Christ died in order that all might be saved, and that He saves all who commit themselves to Him in faith (see sect. VI and chaps. 8, 9 and 10 for this second truth).

1. The universal nature of God's saving purpose is made known in many ways.

The Bible declares that:

(*a*) *It is God's will that all should be saved* (1 Tim. 2: 4; 2 Pet. 3: 9; 1 John 4: 14).

(*b*) *In fulfilment of the divine will, Christ became the Saviour of all men.*

(i) As by the Incarnation He identified Himself with man as man, so by His death He made reconciliation for man's sin (Heb. 2: 9–18).

(ii) The Scripture says Christ ' died for all ' (2 Cor. 5: 15), that He tasted ' death for every man ' (Heb. 2: 9), that he ' gave Himself a ransom for all ' (1 Tim. 2: 6) and that He is ' the Lamb of God, which taketh away the sin of the world ' (John 1: 29). He declared, 'And I, if I be lifted up from the earth, will draw all men unto Me ' (John 12: 32).

(iii) Consequently no ill effect of the Fall is beyond the scope of His redeeming work (Rom. 5: 18; 1 John 3: 8; Isa. 53: 6; Titus 2: 11, R.S.V.; Rom. 5: 20).

   The free justification provided in Christ is offered to all who ' have sinned, and come short of the glory of God ' (Rom. 3: 23, 24, 29).

(iv) His offer and His promise to bestow the blessings of salvation are given to all mankind (Matt. 11: 28; John 7: 37; Rev. 3: 20; 21: 6).

(c) *The blessings of salvation are offered freely and equally to all* (Luke 2: 10, 11; John 3: 16; Acts 10: 43; 1 Tim. 4: 10).

The declaration ' whosoever shall call on the name of the Lord shall be saved ' is a promise given in Old Testament days by Joel (2: 32). Its fulfilment in Christ was announced to the assembled representatives of Israel at Pentecost (Acts 2: 5, 16–21), and to Jew and Gentile generally in Rom. 10: 12, 13. (See also Isa. 42: 6; 45: 22; Acts 13: 47.)

(d) *The Lord Jesus Christ lays upon His followers the duty of carrying the gospel to all mankind* (Luke 24: 46, 47; Matt. 28: 19; Acts 1: 8; 20: 21; 2 Cor. 5: 14, 20).

In this ministry Christ's witnesses are co-workers with the Holy Spirit, who directs their witness and Himself convinces the world of sin, of righteousness and of judgment (John 16: 8).

(e) *Those who are lost receive God's sentence of rejection in spite of the fact that Christ died for them.*

They are lost not because they *could* not, but because they *would* not be saved. They are condemned for ' denying the Lord that bought them ' (2 Pet. 2: 1) and for rejecting the life He offers them (John 5: 40; Matt. 23: 37).

The Epistle to the Hebrews declares the possibility of final rejection of him ' who hath trodden under foot the Son of God, and hath counted the blood of the covenant, wherewith he was sanctified, an unholy thing ' (Heb. 10: 29), and Paul speaks of ' them that perish; because they received not the love of the truth, that they might be saved ' (2 Thess. 2: 10).

2. While the Scripture proclaims so plainly that all men may be saved, there are those who teach that salvation is for ' the elect ' only.

(*a*) Those who thus teach believe that the eternal destiny of each person is determined before he is born. That is to say, while it is God's will that ' the elect ' shall be saved, it is equally His will that the rest of mankind shall be lost. God has chosen who shall and who shall not be saved and His decree is unalterable. The Last Judgment will be the outworking of the divine separation which has existed from the beginning.

Part of this teaching is the claim that the grace bestowed upon ' the elect ' works irresistibly upon them, making sure that they will never fall from their divinely appointed state.

(*b*) Those who hold these beliefs offer no explanation why one man should have been chosen for eternal life and another for eternal death, beyond the suggestion that this action of God must be seen as a demonstration of His sovereign power and of His right to do as He wills with His own creatures.

The thought of God acting in this selective way toward mankind is completely at variance, however, with His character as revealed in Christ, and therefore with the message of the gospel we are charged to proclaim.

3. This idea of ' election ' claims support—wrongly, we hold—from certain passages of Scripture having to do with God's foreknowledge and His predestinating control.

(*a*) The foreknowledge of God does not interfere with the

exercise of man's free will, but is His awareness of the way in which men use this gift and of the ultimate consequences of their actions—see Matt. 23: 36-39, where Christ foresaw and predicted the destruction of Jerusalem, but placed full responsibility for this disaster upon the freely chosen actions of men.

(b) Neither are God's predestinating decisions about man's salvation in conflict with man's freedom of choice in the matter. Predestination has to do with *character*—not with the destiny of particular *individuals*.

God has declared that He is ' no respecter of persons ', but He has shown clearly that He *is* a respecter of *character*. The predestination of the Bible simply signifies God's ordaining or determining beforehand that persons who possess a certain character can enjoy particular blessings, or inherit a particular destiny *for which, because of that character, they are fitted*.

For example, God has predestined or predetermined that sinners confessing and forsaking sin shall obtain mercy; that believers in Jesus Christ shall be saved; that rejecters of Jesus Christ shall perish; that the saints shall enjoy His favour; that those who endure to the end shall have eternal life.

(c) In His dealings with mankind God chose certain individuals for special duty—Jeremiah to be His prophet (1: 5), Saul of Tarsus to be His messenger to the Gentiles (Acts 9: 15) and, above all, Israel to be His people (Deut. 7: 6). But while it was a high privilege to be chosen by God, it was also a very solemn responsibility. Election was never to security but to duty. Nor were those thus chosen singled out because of their own strength or virtue (Deut. 7: 7) but only because God had a work for them to do. If they failed Him, then they lost their privileged place (Rev. 2: 5).

Section VI. THE NEED FOR MAN TO RESPOND TO THE OFFER OF SALVATION

Whosoever will, let him take the water of life freely (Rev. 22:17).

1. The truth that Christ has died for all does not of necessity mean that all men will be saved.

While it is God's desire that His saving purpose should be fulfilled in and through every human life, He is dealing with men to whom He has given freedom of choice in this matter.

No man can be saved against his will. He can welcome or oppose God's redeeming purpose for his life. The Bible presents man's response to the offer of Christ as the greatest exercise of the power of choice that he can make. It is the choice of all choices, a choice between life and death.

2. The full benefits brought to men by the sacrifice of Christ are received only by those who identify themselves with Him.

God's purpose is that men should be born again and bear His likeness. Thus, as well as reconciling them to Himself, He imparts His regenerating Spirit and equips them to live as His children.

The redeeming work of Christ is related to the whole of this purpose and involves both what He does *for* men and what He can do *in* them. Both are necessary.

The victory Christ won for man over the power of evil does not exempt believers from their own encounter with temptation. But He who won the victory *for* them can demonstrate His triumph *within* them (see John 16: 33; 17: 15; Rom. 8: 36, 37; Eph. 6: 10–12).

Section VII. THE NEED FOR THE PROCLAMATION OF THE GOSPEL

1. The gospel must be made known.

Although ' the same Lord is Lord of all and bestows His riches upon all who call upon Him . . . how are men to call upon Him in whom they have not believed? And how are they to believe in Him of whom they have never heard? And how are they to hear without a preacher? ' (Rom. 10: 12, 14, R.S.V.).

Paul supplied the answer to his own questions in verse 17: ' Faith comes from what is heard, and what is heard comes by the preaching of Christ.'

2. The Holy Spirit equips men to proclaim the salvation which they themselves have accepted.

(See chap. 5, sect. IV, para. 3 (*f*).)

(*a*) *The Holy Spirit uses those who are converted in this ministry of persuasion* (2 Cor. 5: 18–20).

By means of this ministry the world has been given

    (i) the Scriptures,

   (ii) many writings which expound the gospel and preserve the history of its impact on mankind,

  (iii) the institution of many organized efforts for the propagation of the gospel, and

  (iv) the continuing ministry of Christian witness.

(*b*) *Every Christian is called to this commitment which should include*

    (i) a working faith that all men can be saved (1 Tim. 2: 1–6; Matt. 9: 36–38),

   (ii) the support of every means whereby the gospel can be proclaimed, and

  (iii) personal witness for Christ.

(See also chaps. 8–10 for the Holy Spirit's work in imparting the blessings of salvation.)

3. Many have never been confronted with the gospel of God's salvation.

(*a*) *Theirs is not the unwillingness of unbelief, but ignorance of the message of salvation.*

They are free from the guilt of those who, having heard the gospel, have rejected it.

(b) *Their lack of knowledge of the way of salvation is no sign that God does not care for them.*

To them, as with all mankind, He ' giveth . . . life, and breath, and all things ', and is ' not far from every one of us: for in Him we live, and move, and have our being ' (Acts 17: 25, 27, 28).

He is their Creator, Preserver and Governor. They are within the embrace of His love and the scope of His grace (Acts 10: 34, 35).

(c) *None is without some measure of light* (Rom. 1: 20).

(d) *They will be held accountable before God for the response they make to the light they have been given.*

Those who know nothing of Christ or of Bible teaching will be judged by ' the law written in their hearts ' (Rom. 2: 15).

> Who will render to every man according to his deeds . . . for there is no respect of persons with God. For as many as have sinned without the law shall also perish without law: and as many as have sinned in the law shall be judged by the law (Rom. 2: 6, 11, 12).

In accountability for their response to the light given, they stand on common ground with all men. This same rule applies to all, which means that those who have received most light carry the greatest responsibility. ' Unto whomsoever much is given, of him shall be much required ' (Luke 12: 48). (See also Matt. 11: 20–24; 12: 41, 42.)

(e) *The continuing need to spread the gospel is a solemn challenge to believers everywhere.*

All men need the gospel and have a right to hear it. It is our duty to take it to them (1 Cor. 9: 16).

8

SALVATION RECEIVED

' We believe that repentance toward God, faith in our Lord Jesus Christ, and regeneration by the Holy Spirit are necessary to salvation ' (Article 7).

' We believe that we are justified by grace, through faith in our Lord Jesus Christ; and that he that believeth hath the witness in himself ' (Article 8).

Section I. INTRODUCTION

1. Articles 7, 8, 9 and 10 are concerned with one subject— salvation as a personal experience.

(*a*) Taken together these Articles provide an exposition of the words ' whosoever *will* may be *saved* ' (Article 6), as they speak of

> (i) *the blessings which salvation imparts*—regeneration by the Holy Spirit, justification by grace, the inward witness to salvation, the maintenance of the experience leading to sanctification;
>
> (ii) *the way in which salvation can be received*—by repentance toward God, faith in our Lord Jesus Christ and continued obedient faith in Christ.

(*b*) When combined with Article 11, Articles 7 to 10 show that the experience of salvation is related to time in three ways. There is

> (i) *an initial experience* (Articles 7 and 8)—that of conversion (Eph. 1: 12, 13);
>
> (ii) *a continuing experience* (Articles 9 and 10)—the new life maintained and developed (2 Pet. 3: 18); and
>
> (iii) *an ultimate experience* (Article 11)—salvation's transforming purpose fully effected (1 John 3: 2).

(c) Articles 7 and 8 are taken together in this chapter because they both deal with the experience of receiving salvation, speaking first of the response to be made to God, and then of the blessings received by him who thus repents and believes.

2. Repentance toward God and faith in our Lord Jesus Christ are necessary to salvation.

Testifying both to the Jews, and also to the Greeks, repentance toward God, and faith toward our Lord Jesus Christ (Acts 20: 21).

(a) These two phrases taken together describe the action of the seeker who turns to God for salvation. He who acts thus is repentant and believing at the same time; his repentance is a *believing* repentance and his faith is that of a *repenting* soul.

(b) In speaking of repentance and faith as being acts of *man* set over against regeneration, justification and sanctification as being acts of *God*, it is vital to guard against the error that the initiative in repentance and faith lies with the seeker. Saving repentance and faith are responses by the soul to the light and love which comes from God. God is not gracious because a man repents and believes; a man repents and believes because he is persuaded that God is gracious irrespective of any human action. Grace is God's *undeserved* favour expressed in *seeking* as well as *saving* grace.

(c) But man can resist and refuse to respond. If he will not repent, God neither compels him nor does his repenting for him. Repenting and believing depend upon the combined action of both God and man.

Section II.   REPENTANCE TOWARD GOD

1. Repentance is the sincere determination to forsake sin and obey God.

The word ' repentance ' is not necessarily a religious expression, but is a translation of Hebrew and Greek words which mean changing one's mind or turning from one thing to another. Thus, when used of the sinner seeking salvation, it means that he who has hitherto clung to sin changes his mind and determines, by the help of God, to act in the opposite manner.

However, both the Bible and experience show that there is a form of repentance for wrongdoing which is not ' toward God ' and not unto salvation. 2 Cor. 7: 10 speaks of a ' godly sorrow ' which ' worketh repentance to salvation ', and of a ' sorrow of the world ' which ' worketh death '.

2. Genuine repentance includes:

(*a*) *Conviction of sin*. The penitent recognizes that he is guilty and deserving of punishment.

> Against Thee, Thee only, have I sinned, and done this evil in Thy sight (Ps. 51: 4; see also Gen. 42: 21; Ps. 38: 4).

(*b*) *Hatred of sin*. He turns against the sin which he formerly loved, realizing it to be evil in the sight of God, and condemning himself for committing it.

> They shall lothe themselves for the evils which they have committed in all their abominations. And they shall know that I am the Lord (Ezek. 6: 9, 10).

(*c*) *Sorrow for sin, or contrition*. He regrets his wrongdoing, and wishes he had not acted so shamefully toward so loving a God. His sorrow is for *sin itself*, not merely for its *consequences*.

> Godly grief produces a repentance that leads to salvation and brings no regret, but worldly grief produces death (2 Cor. 7: 10, R.S.V.; see also Ps. 38: 18; Matt. 26: 75).

In the quoted verse *godly grief* means sorrow for having sinned against God, while *worldly grief* is sorrow without faith in God, or mere regret for the consequences of sin.

(*d*) *Renunciation of sin*. He is willing there and then and for ever to give up the sinful ways and doings which he regrets. If a sinner is unwilling for this, and if he does not actually intend to give up wrongdoing as far as he can, his repentance is insincere.

Let the wicked forsake his way, and the unrighteous man his thoughts: and let him return unto the Lord, and He will have mercy upon him (Isa. 55: 7).

Willingness to give up sin does not necessarily imply *power* to do so. Power comes with salvation. A drowning man may be *willing* to be saved in any way possible, yet be utterly without *power* to save himself, or even to rid himself of hindrances to his being saved. Just so a man may be perfectly willing to let God save him in His own way, although quite unable to do anything toward saving himself.

(*e*) *Confession of sin.* The true penitent makes a full confession of his sins *to God.* He is also willing to acknowledge his sinfulness before men, and to confess to others wherein he has wronged them.

He that covereth his sins shall not prosper: but whoso confesseth and forsaketh them shall have mercy (Prov. 28: 13; see also Luke 15: 21).

(*f*) *Desire for forgiveness.* The penitent longs for pardon, and it is this which prompts him to repent.

Have mercy upon me, O God, according to Thy lovingkindness: according unto the multitude of Thy tender mercies blot out my transgressions (Ps. 51: 1; see also Ps. 25: 11; Luke 18: 13).

(*g*) *Submission to God.* He yields or surrenders himself to God, willing to obey and please Him in everything.

Be ye not stiffnecked . . . but yield yourselves unto the Lord (2 Chron. 30: 8; see also Acts 9: 6).

(*h*) *Willingness to make restitution.* The penitent endeavours to put right, as far as he can, any wrong that he has done.

Zacchaeus . . . said . . . Behold, Lord, the half of my goods I give to the poor; and if I have taken any thing from any man by false accusation, I restore him fourfold (Luke 19: 8; see also Num. 5: 7).

Repentance comes before the realization of forgiveness. If God forgave unrepentant sinners He would do them positive injury by encouraging and hardening them in their sin. A wise father would refuse to forgive and be reconciled until his disobedient child had shown that he was sorry and had promised not to offend again. God acts in the same way.

We should not be misled about feelings. One man's repentance may be linked with feelings of deep penitence; another may show signs of great relief and release; while yet another may come to God with conflicting emotions or even without much feeling at all. Repentance is not complete until it goes beyond feelings, or even confession. Decisions must be translated into action. This means that a sinner could be repenting in part for months or years before he comes to the point of saying the required 'yes' to God.

Section III. FAITH IN OUR LORD JESUS CHRIST

> With the heart man believeth unto righteousness; and with the mouth confession is made unto salvation (Rom. 10: 10).

1. Saving faith is that act of trust by which the sinner enters into the relationship with God known as 'being saved'.

(a) In common usage faith means 'believing, trusting in, putting reliance upon someone or something deemed to be trustworthy'—a human reaction that has many expressions in everyday life.

(b) In Christian conversion the word faith is all-important (Heb. 11: 6). Some people never receive salvation because they never come to the point of believing that God will be as good as His word.

(c) Faith which is 'saving faith' is that act of personal trust by which the sinner commits himself to God and accepts as his own the salvation which God so freely offers.

2. Saving faith has certain distinguishing features.

(a) It is a *personal* faith.

The gospel revelation and promises, given to all, are appropriated for one's self—' Who loved *me*, and gave Himself for *me* ' (Gal. 2: 20).

(b) It is a faith that *looks to God, and to Him alone*.

The trusting soul no longer relies on anyone but God. Faith must be directed toward Him alone.

(c) It is a faith that *arises in response to the gospel message* (Rom. 10: 17; Eph. 1: 13).

He who would be saved believes in the grace of God as revealed in Christ, and not in any personal works of righteousness (Titus 3: 4–6). This is an aspect of the gospel emphasized by the words which define faith as being ' in our Lord Jesus Christ ', and by the truth that ' we are justified by grace through faith in our Lord Jesus Christ ' (Article 8; see sect. IV, para. 2).

(d) Saving faith must be *accompanied by repentance*.

' If I regard iniquity in my heart, the Lord will not hear me ' (Ps. 66: 18), but ' if our hearts condemn us not, then have we confidence toward God ' (1 John 3: 21).

Faith is described in Article 9 as ' *obedient* faith in Christ '. A ' disobedient faith ' would be self-contradictory. The Bible condemns the error of those who suppose that God will receive them while still clinging to their sin (Isa. 29: 13; Jer. 7: 3–10; Hos. 6: 4–6; Amos 5: 21–24; Mark 7: 6; Jas. 4: 4–10; 1 John 2: 4).

(e) It is a faith which *results in committal*.

There is a distinction between *intellectual* faith and faith *in action*. *Intellectual* faith is believing with the mind, being convinced that something is true; faith *in action* does this and more— it acts upon this conviction. The former is ineffective when it stands alone (Jas. 2: 14–20). Thus saving faith moves beyond intellectual belief to the point where the believer says, ' I am trusting Thee *now* '. Saving faith is a *present* and *committing* faith.

3. Faith has a twofold expression—in passivity (resting on God's promises) and by activity (going forward to do His will).

Faith is expressed in relation to

(a) the saving work of God in Christ, as a *trusting* repose which 'worketh not, but believeth on Him that justifieth the ungodly' (Rom. 4: 5);

(b) the work of grace God has promised to do in us, by *believing prayer* that waits on Him for the fulfilment of His promises;

(c) His requirements in terms of dedication and service, by *acts of trusting obedience*.

4. Notable examples of repentance and faith are found

(a) *in the penitential Psalms*—especially 32, 38, 51 and 130; and

(b) *in the two accounts of what repentance meant for Paul*—in his turning from unbelief in Christ (Acts 9: 1-20; 22: 6-16) and from trust in his own righteousness (Phil. 3: 7-12).

Section IV. BLESSINGS BROUGHT BY SALVATION —JUSTIFICATION

1. These are justification by grace, regeneration by the Holy Spirit, and the witness within or assurance of salvation.

(a) All are part of the one experience of salvation yet are named separately to show

      (i) that the work of salvation provides a remedy for sin in all its aspects;

      (ii) that salvation means both a change in man's relationship with God (justification), and a change in man himself; he is ' born again ' (regeneration);

      (iii) those who believe in Christ the blessings they can expect.

(*b*) The comprehensive nature of salvation includes adoption into the family of God and leads on to sanctification or full salvation.

(*c*) Although justification, regeneration and assurance are part of the one spiritual experience, it is doctrinally correct to speak first of justification by grace. This establishes a new relationship with God which is basic to the spiritual life. God does not justify a man because he is regenerated, but because of his faith in the atoning Saviour.

2. Man is justified by grace through faith in our Lord Jesus Christ.

(*a*) This is the means whereby guilty sinners are reconciled to God. The Bible presents

- (i) examples of the doctrine being proclaimed;
- (ii) testimony by those who know justification as a personal experience; and
- (iii) expositions of the meaning of the doctrine (see the Epistles to the Galatians and Rom. 3: 24 and on through chapters 4 and 5, and 10: 3–17).

(*b*) To be 'justified' means to be declared 'just' or 'right' in the eyes of the law, and is used in describing the relationship of man to human as well as to divine law.

In the Bible the word 'justification' is closely connected with the word 'righteousness', and in New Testament Greek they share a common root. When Paul speaks in Phil. 3: 9 and in Rom. 3: 22 of 'the righteousness which is of God by faith', he is dealing with the same doctrine.

(*c*) Justification by grace needs to be defined.

The Bible speaks of two ways in which men seek to be justified before God:

> Through this man [the Saviour, Jesus] is preached unto you the forgiveness of sins: and by Him all that believe are justified from all things, from which ye could not be justified by the law of Moses (Acts 13: 38, 39).

A man is not justified by the works of the law, but by the faith of Jesus Christ . . . for by the works of the law shall no flesh be justified (Gal. 2: 16).

Here the contrast is between being justified by the works of the law and by faith in Jesus.

The former is called legal justification, and its principle is stated in Deut. 25: 1:

They shall justify the righteous, and condemn the wicked.

The second is known variously as ' Christian ', ' salvation ', ' evangelical ' or ' gospel ' justification, and is described in Rom. 4: 5:

To him who worketh not, but believeth on Him that justifieth the ungodly, his faith is counted for righteousness.

The contrast lies in:

(i) *The difference in the character of those who receive it.* Legal justification is for the innocent; Christian justification is for the guilty.

(ii) *The difference in the reason for justification.* In legal justification the accused is declared ' just ' on his own merit, because he is seen to be innocent. In Christian justification the accused is declared free from condemnation by reason of his penitent faith in Christ. He fully admits his guilt but is justified by the pardoning mercy of God.

The first is a claim of desert (what is deserved or earned); the second is the claim of faith in the atoning Saviour.

The contrast between the two is absolute in our dealings with God. No man can claim both. To claim one means abandoning any claim to the other. This is the message of the Epistle to the Galatians:

If righteousness come by the law, then Christ is dead in vain (Gal. 2: 21).

Christ is become of no effect unto you, whosoever of you are justified by the law (Gal. 5: 4).

Justification by grace through faith in Christ is the one way of salvation open to men as none can claim to be just of himself (Gal. 3: 22).

3. Justification is spoken of sometimes as an act of God's mercy and sometimes as an act of His justice.

(a) The *mercy of God* is displayed by the grace which has given to men an atoning Saviour (1 John 4: 10).

(b) The *justice of God* is seen in His act of justifying those who present this all-prevailing plea.

Thus in 1 John 1: 9 the forgiveness and cleansing given to those who confess their sins is seen as a demonstration both of the *faithfulness* and the *justice* of God.

4. Those who are justified recognize that they are sinners before God in common with all mankind.

No one receiving this provision of grace can separate himself from the rest of mankind. None can say ' I thank Thee, that I am not as other men are '. He remains ' only a sinner, saved by grace '.

Men must observe this identification with others at all times. He who receives pardon must allow his new relationship with God to transform his relationship with men; he who receives mercy must show mercy (Matt. 5: 7; 6: 12, 14, 15; 18: 21–35; Luke 17: 3, 4; Eph. 4: 32; Col. 3: 13; Jas. 2: 12, 13).

5. Justification means that man is restored to fellowship with God.

Consequently

(a) the forgiven sinner finds himself free from the condemnation of the law (Rom. 8: 1);

(b) he enjoys God's favour (Rom. 5: 1); and

(c) he is continually humbled by the cost of forgiveness (1 Pet. 2: 24).

6. At the same time, forgiveness cannot make the past as if it had never been, nor wholly undo its consequences.

(*a*) Earthly blessings—health, reputation, friends—lost by sinning are not automatically restored, though they may in part be regained by right living.

(*b*) The effect of sinning upon the lives of others may remain even after the sinner himself has been forgiven. He should, by God's help, do what he can to remedy this effect.

Section V.   BLESSINGS BROUGHT BY SALVATION —REGENERATION BY THE HOLY SPIRIT

1. Regeneration is one of the words used to describe the great change God the Holy Spirit works in those whose sins are forgiven.

(*a*) Regeneration means ' re-birth ' or ' the coming of new life '. In New Testament days the word was used to describe such events as the renewal of plant life in the springtime. In Christian doctrine it is used to describe the spiritual rebirth that salvation brings to those who believe in Jesus as Saviour.

(*b*) Teaching about this spiritual change is concerned with both its immediate and its subsequent effect. This means that regeneration, adoption and sanctification have to be studied singly and in their relation to each other. Together they show how God's salvation meets the need of the awakened sinner, not only on account of his sinful state before God but on account of his sinful nature.

Seeing that the life of the Christian after conversion is referred to in Articles 9 and 10, this chapter deals only with the initial change produced by the coming of new life to the soul.

2. The revolutionary nature of this change is revealed by the words used to describe it.

It is spoken of as:

(*a*) *Becoming a new creature* (2 Cor. 5: 17; Gal. 6: 15).

There is not just a reform of what was there already, but something as distinctly new as is brought about by any other creative act of God.

(b) *Being born anew*, ' born of the Spirit ' (John 3: 6; see also John 3: 7; 1 Pet. 1: 23).

The word ' regeneration ' (Titus 3: 5) does not appear in some translations of the Bible, but there are many references to being born of God and becoming His children.

This implies a new start, a new nature, a new relationship and a new likeness—truths which are emphasized still further by the teaching concerning adoption.

(c) *Passing from death to life*—a spiritual resurrection (John 5: 24; 1 John 3: 14).

(d) *Passing from darkness to light* (John 8: 12; Eph. 5: 8; 1 Thess. 5: 5).

(e) *Receiving eternal life* (John 17: 2; Rom. 6: 23).

Here the word ' eternal ' is used to describe a life which has the nature and qualities of the life that is to come, and is defined by Jesus as knowing God and having fellowship with Him through the Son (John 17: 3; 1 John 5: 20).

(f) *Becoming the temple of the indwelling Spirit* (1 Cor. 6: 19).

(g) *Receiving of Christian virtues, notably love, faith and hope* (Gal. 5: 6; Rom. 5: 5).

3. The revolutionary nature of this change is seen in the means by which it is effected.

(a) It is brought about by the Holy Spirit working in the power of the atonement, that is, in the power of the risen Saviour (compare John 7: 39 with Acts 2: 32, 33).

(b) The Spirit who indwells the heart is He who is undivided in essence with the Father and with the Son.

Thus there is frequent reference to Christ dwelling in the hearts of believers, as in Eph. 3: 16, 17: ' That He would grant you, according to the riches of His glory, to be strengthened with might by His Spirit in the inner man; that Christ may dwell in your hearts by faith '; and in Col. 1: 27: ' Christ in you, the hope of glory '. It is also ' God which worketh in you both to will and to do of His good pleasure ' (Phil. 2: 13).

4. The beginning of this ' good work ' in men (Phil. 1: 6) is related to its ultimate purpose.

God's eternal purpose is to draw men into fellowship with Himself so that they may be conformed to His likeness (Gen. 1: 26; 1 John 3: 2).

5. The work of regeneration in the soul is beyond human understanding.

This is a doctrine which though difficult to explain, finds its ultimate proof in personal experience.

> The wind bloweth where it listeth, and thou hearest the sound thereof, but canst not tell whence it cometh, and whither it goeth: so is every one that is born of the Spirit (John 3: 8).

> Unto Him that is able to do exceedingly abundantly above all that we ask or think, according to the power that worketh in us (Eph. 3: 20).

6. Regeneration and Sanctification

Sanctification is closely connected with regeneration, for both are concerned with the work of the Holy Spirit, who makes men the children of God both in name and in the likeness of His holy nature (see 1 Pet. 1: 14–16).

Although sanctification is the subject of chapter 10, it is mentioned here to draw attention to the truth that the spiritual change known as conversion is the root of all subsequent development in Christian character.

It is clear that:

(a) *The redeeming work of Jesus has sanctifying purpose and releases sanctifying power* (1 Cor. 1: 30; Titus 2: 13, 14; Heb. 10: 10).

(*b*) *God's sanctifying purpose is a necessary part of the gospel call* (2 Thess. 2: 13).

Paul was sent to the Gentiles

> To open their eyes, and to turn them from darkness to light and from the power of Satan unto God, that they may receive forgiveness of sins, and inheritance among them which are sanctified by faith that is in Me (Acts 26: 18).

Section VI.   BLESSINGS BROUGHT BY SALVATION —ADOPTION INTO THE FAMILY OF GOD

Adoption is that act by which God receives the pardoned and regenerated sinner into His family.

1. By this act of saving grace men are brought into a relationship with God as Father that is not theirs by natural birth.

(*a*) Because God is the Creator of human life, all men are His ' offspring ' (Acts 17: 24–29). But the right to be called a *son* or a *child* of God in the spiritual sense is reserved for those who receive salvation through Christ (John 1: 12 , 13).

By conversion man's will, which had been enslaved, is released so that the child of God becomes a responsible person in a sense higher than ever he was before.

> You are therefore no longer a slave but a son, and if a son, then also by God's own act an heir (Gal. 4: 7, N.E.B.).

(*b*) Only as men receive Jesus Christ as Saviour is the eternal purpose of God concerning their sonship realized in individual experience (Gal. 3: 26; 4: 4, 5; Eph. 1: 4, 5).

(*c*) As the Father is also King, the act that makes a man a son of God makes him also a citizen of the Kingdom (Eph. 2: 19).

2. Adoption brings each new member of the heavenly family into spiritual union with all other children of God.

This union in Christ binds men and women in a closer and

more enduring relationship than that of any other human tie
(Gal. 3: 28; Rom. 12: 3–5; 1 Cor. 12: 12–20; Eph. 2: 16–22;
4: 1–16; 1 Pet. 2: 4–10).

3. Adoption bestows a glorious inheritance.

(*a*) The full glory of this inheritance can be measured only
by the infinite nature of God Himself. Scriptural language speaks
of blessings ' according to God's grace ', and ' according to His
glory ', of being ' heirs of God, and joint-heirs with Christ '
(Rom. 8: 17), of the ' unsearchable riches of Christ ', and of
receiving all blessings in and with Him (Rom. 8: 32; Eph. 1: 3).

(*b*) The treasures of this wealth are made known in God's
word, and by the Holy Spirit's illumination of the soul (1 Cor. 2:
9, 10; Eph. 1: 15–18).

(*c*) The greatest revelation is that adoption brings men into a
special relationship with

    (i) *the Father*.

        Jesus said to Mary, Go to My brethren, and say unto
them, I ascend unto My Father, and your Father ' (John
20: 17).

        In Jas. 1: 17 God is described as the Father of
lights, from whom comes every good and perfect
gift, and whose unceasing care for His children is
contrasted with the imperfections of the best of
human parents (Luke 11: 13).

    (ii) *the Son*.

        By His incarnation and atonement Jesus so
identified Himself with men that He is one with
those who receive His saving grace and ' is not
ashamed to call them brethren ' (Heb. 2: 11).

        He bestows the inestimable inheritance of sharing
His glory (John 12: 26; 14: 3; Rom. 8: 17; Eph. 1:
11) and of sharing the love the Father bears to the
Son (John 17: 24, 26) and the Son bears to the
Father (John 15: 9).

(iii) *the Holy Spirit*, who works in the soul with the power that raised Christ from the dead to the throne of supreme glory (Rom. 8: 11; Eph. 1: 19–23).

(*d*) The full ' manifestation of the sons of God ' belongs also to the future. Thus there is a call for a faith that will appropriate present blessings, and for a hope that believes for those which are to come (Rom. 8: 18–25).

Section VII. BLESSINGS BROUGHT BY SALVATION —ASSURANCE

Assurance of salvation is the knowledge of forgiveness and acceptance which God Himself gives to the saved soul.

This divine witness is given by the Spirit of God and is confirmed by experience.

1. The Holy Spirit gives inward witness in a twofold way

(*a*) *He causes men to know Christ as a present personal Saviour.*

The words of Article 8, ' he that believeth hath the witness in himself ', are taken from 1 John 5: 10, which speaks of the work of the Spirit of Truth, who makes a man aware that Jesus is the Christ, the Son of God and giver of eternal life. Although a man may have heard the gospel message many times, by this inner illumination he now knows it to be true, and true for him personally.

With this knowledge of Christ as a personal Saviour comes the confidence to claim every spiritual blessing Christ bestows (Heb. 4: 16; 10: 19–22).

(*b*) *The Holy Spirit gives inward witness of adoption* (Rom. 8: 15; Gal. 4: 6).

(*c*) *These two aspects of divine witness complement each other.*

The first assures the believer that *he is in a state of grace*; the second that *the work of grace has been done within him*. While these two testimonies are distinct in thought, they may well be simultaneous and unified in experience, and in this union with Christ is the pledge for this world and the next of ' all things that pertain unto life and godliness ' (2 Pet. 1: 3).

2. The witness of the Spirit is confirmed by the testimony of a changed life.

Following his conversion, the seeker is made aware of the transformation this inward change effects in his outward attitudes and conduct.

The First Epistle of John is concerned almost entirely with the witness to salvation which is given by the changed life:

> These things have I written unto you that believe on the name of the Son of God; that ye may know that ye have eternal life (5: 13).

The words ' we know ' or ' hereby we know ' appear repeatedly to introduce statements concerning the means whereby men may be assured that they are born again, are children of God, are passed from death to life, that God dwells in them and they in Him. These statements unite in emphasizing the teaching that the conduct of the children of God will bear the marks of the divine nature.

3. Assurance is further confirmed by progress in Christian living.

(a) Growth in grace will open a believer's heart and mind to the ' full wealth of conviction that understanding brings ' (Col. 2: 2, N.E.B.).

(b) Experience of divine guidance will confirm that one's life is under God's control (2 Cor. 1: 10).

(c) The fruit of the Spirit manifest in the development of Christian character will give assurance of the continued working of the divine life in transforming power (John 15: 1, 2, 5).

SALVATION MAINTAINED

' We believe that continuance in a state of salvation depends upon continued obedient faith in Christ ' (Article 9).

Section I. INTRODUCTION

Articles 9 and 10 deal with the development of Christian life after conversion. They are complementary in the sense that Article 10 is concerned with the deeper work of grace that *God* wills to do, while Article 9 deals with the co-operating response *man* must continue to give.

This latter subject—the life a Christian convert should lead and the principles that should guide him in his walk with God—is dealt with

(*a*) in such sentences as:

Abide in Me, and I in you (John 15: 4).

If we live in the Spirit, let us also walk in the Spirit (Gal. 5: 25).

As ye have therefore received Christ Jesus the Lord, so walk ye in Him (Col. 2: 6).

Grow in grace, and in the knowledge of our Lord and Saviour Jesus Christ (2 Pet. 3: 18).

Little children, abide in Him (1 John 2: 28).

(*b*) in such passages as: Phil. 2: 12, 13; Titus 2: 11–14; 1 Pet. 1: 1–9; 1 John 2: 24; Jude 20, 21. Col. 1: 9–14 provides a prayer for Christian converts, and 1: 21–23; 2: 6–8 give accompanying exhortation and warning.

The heart of this teaching is that the Christian life requires a continued commitment to Christ as Saviour and Lord—that is, a life of combined faith and obedience. Where this is not maintained then backsliding—to a greater or lesser degree—inevitably follows.

Section II. CONTINUED OBEDIENT FAITH IN CHRIST

1. The faith God's people should continually exercise is of the same nature as saving faith.

Just as the sinner commits himself to God, trusting Him for promised salvation, so the saved soul commits himself to God, trusting Him for promised help and keeping.

(a) It is *faith in the God of grace revealed in Christ*—the trust which relies upon God and rests upon His faithfulness (1 Pet. 5: 7; 1 Cor. 10: 13; Heb. 13: 5, 6; Jude 24, 25).

(b) It is *continued* faith in Christ—the faith of *constant* dependence (1 John 5: 11, 12).

(c) It is a faith that produces *obedience to God's will*. One of the purposes of the death of Jesus was to enable men to keep the law of God (Rom. 8: 3, 4; 1 John 5: 3).

(d) It is a *co-operating* faith, which enables God's children to work with Him toward the realization of His revealed purposes (1 John 3: 2, 3; Phil. 3: 12–14; Heb. 12: 1, 2).

(e) It is a *venturing* faith, which began by stepping out in trust that God would do as He had promised and which continues so to do, particularly in regard to calls to special service. For example, Acts 10: 28, 29; 13: 2, 3; Phil. 4: 13.

(f) It is a *growing* faith, strengthened each time it is exercised.

2. Continuance in a state of salvation calls for continued obedience.

(a) *Those who disobey the revealed will of God are, by the measure of their disobedience, falling from grace* (Luke 6: 46; Matt. 7: 26, 27; Rom. 2: 6–11; 6: 16).

It is the obedient to whom salvation is given (Heb. 5: 9; John 15: 14; 1 John 2: 3, 4, N.E.B.).

(b) *The child of God will continue to be responsive to the leading of the Holy Spirit* (Rom. 8: 14).

(c) *Obedience is the nature of the new life.*

(i) God's children pray for His will to be done on earth, and offer themselves that this prayer may be answered in and through them.

(ii) The transforming life that comes from the risen Saviour gives the power to obey (Rom. 8: 3, 4).

(iii) A dutiful heart is part of the blessing bestowed by the new covenant (Jer. 31: 33; Ezek. 36: 26, 27).

(iv) Christian obedience works by love (John 14: 15; 1 John 5: 3).

(v) All who possess the Spirit of Christ manifest His obedience to the divine will (John 6: 38; Phil. 2: 5).

3. The continued obedient faith God requires involves both divine and human action.

(a) The desire and power to serve God comes with the change of heart wrought by the Holy Spirit at conversion (para. 2(c)).

(b) The continued obedient faith required is dependent not only on this change of heart but on the continued inward working of the Holy Spirit (Phil. 2: 13; Heb. 13: 20, 21).

God does not impart to His children any spiritual change that would make them independent of Him. There is no way of maintaining a state of grace that sets aside the command of Jesus to abide in Him.

(c) Continued obedient faith also involves human action. God requires our continual obedience to all that His Spirit urges us to do (Phil. 2: 12, 13).

Such passages as Jas. 2: 14–26; Matt. 21: 28–31 and 1 John 3: 17, 18 show that the Christian graces become meaningful only as they are expressed in action.

(d) God's children live in a world where every Christian grace is challenged; they are tried as by fire (John 16: 33; 2 Tim. 3: 12).

The triumph of God can be proved in these testings. What

could lead to the extinction of Christian trust can become the means by which faith is strengthened and Christian character developed (Rom. 5: 3–5; 1 Pet. 1: 6, 7; 5: 8–10; Jas. 1: 2–4).

Some aspects of Christian character are produced only by such encounter with difficulty. This was the way of the Master (Heb. 12: 3). Christ is the supreme example of continued obedient faith, yet of Him it is written, ' Though He were a Son, yet learned He obedience by the things which He suffered ' (Heb. 5: 8).

4. Christian discipleship requires constant co-operation with God for the realization of His purposes.

(a) This includes the recognition that He wills to do

    (i) a work of grace *for* His children—by which they are forgiven, reconciled and justified;

    (ii) a work of grace *within* them—by which their nature is transformed by His regenerating, sanctifying Spirit; and

    (iii) a work of grace *with* or *through* them—by which the change in their lives displays the power and grace of His salvation (Matt. 5: 16; Phil. 2: 14, 15; 1 Pet. 2: 9, 12). Thus they can spread the news of salvation for all by confession of Christ and proclamation of His gospel (Matt. 10: 32, 33; Acts 1: 8); and they can manifest the Spirit of Christ in service to the Christian fellowship and to all men (Gal. 6: 10; Matt. 5: 43–48; 7: 12; 25: 40).

(b) Believers should therefore

    (i) *seek to know God's will*—by prayer, Bible reading, the guidance of the Holy Spirit, the experience of other believers and the challenge of events. In all this it should be remembered that obedience to what is already known opens the way for further revelation.

    (ii) *live a life of prayerful dependence*, that waits on God for grace and power to *be* and to *do* what He wills (2 Cor. 4: 7; 12: 9, 10; Eph. 6: 18).

(iii) *dedicate themselves to godly living*, which abhors ' that
which is evil ', and cleaves ' to that which is good '
(Rom. 12: 9).

This involves a separation in heart, thought and
act from ungodly pursuits, from ungodly attitudes to
life (Rom. 12: 2; 1 John 2: 15, 16) and from ' fleshly
lusts, which war against the soul ' (1 Pet. 2: 11), and
means living ' soberly, righteously, and godly, in this
present world ' (Titus 2: 12), yielding all their
powers as ' instruments of righteousness unto God '
(Rom. 6: 13; see also 12: 1).

In matters of doubt Christian action is governed
by principles set forth in such passages as Rom. 14
and 1 Cor. 8; 10: 24–33.

Section III. BACKSLIDING AND REJECTION—THE RESULT OF FAILURE TO MAINTAIN OBEDIENT FAITH IN CHRIST

1. Backsliding is a scriptural word which describes the falling away of the soul from God after having been saved.

(*a*) A man who falls away from Christian profession but who
has never been truly saved cannot be said to backslide in the
sense of this definition. Nevertheless.

(i) some truly converted people have fallen from grace,
and

(ii) the danger of doing so threatens every Christian.

(*b*) The word ' backsliding ' is used in a twofold sense to
describe

(i) an ultimate experience, when a soul has entirely
departed from God and lost all spiritual life, and

(ii) the process by which this state is reached.

Backsliding is often *secret* at first, being known only to the soul
itself; later it becomes *open*, being seen in the outward life.

(*c*) *Backsliding is an expression of unresponsiveness or opposition to the will of God.*

(*d*) *This arises in the backslider's own heart and will* (Prov. 4: 23).

He begins to decline where, as a seeker, he began to advance—in his personal response to the call of God. At some point in his experience where formerly he said ' yes ' he now says ' no ' to the divine will.

A wrong act is not of itself backsliding; the all-important matter is the *attitude of heart* which accompanies and follows the sinful action. If there is penitence, then forgiveness can be sought and obtained, but if backsliding continues, then an increasing measure of separation from God inevitably follows.

2. The cause of failure can be either in the backslider's faith or in his obedience.

(*a*) *There can be a decline of faith*—a ceasing to trust in Christ as Saviour—

   (i) by relying on some other ground of faith (see Gal. 1: 6—this form of backsliding can affect whole communities as well as individuals), or

   (ii) by abandoning all trust in the gospel message, and making a ' shipwreck ' of faith (1 Tim. 1: 19) by the act of an ' evil heart of unbelief ' which departs from the living God (Heb. 3: 12).

(*b*) *There can be a reversal of conduct by sins of omission or of commission*—failure to use the means of grace, to confess Christ before men, to respond to a call to consecration and service, or the deliberate and continuous practice of wrong conduct in thought and deed (1 Cor. 3: 16, 17; compare 9: 25–27) or a decision to abandon all attempts to live a Christian life (2 Pet. 2: 20–22).

3. At what point can backsliding be said to be entire?

There are two main answers to this question, for the cause can be either a crisis decision or a process of spiritual neglect.

(a) *Backsliding is entire when a man consciously reverses his committal to Christ.*

He will know he is backslidden when

(i) he rejects the demands of Christian discipleship (the *backsliding of disobedience*) or

(ii) he consciously rejects Christ as Saviour (the *backsliding of unbelief*).

This act of Christ-rejection sometimes is called apostasy, a word which means ' to turn one's back upon ', to ' reject ' or ' rebel against ' (Heb. 10: 29; 6: 6).

(b) *Backsliding is entire when all conscious spiritual dealings with God have ceased.*

This state can be reached without any act of apostasy, and without any open separation from Christian profession.

The Bible speaks of backsliders in heart who still profess allegiance to Christ and His Church. Of them it was said, ' Though you have a name for being alive, you are dead ' (Rev. 3: 1, N.E.B.). This is the backsliding that results from continued neglect to maintain the spiritual life (see John 15: 1–6; Heb. 2: 1–4).

In contrast to open apostasy such backsliders may be unaware of their true condition, especially when their decline has not been accompanied by any particular expression of wrongdoing. This state of spiritual death may even co-exist with feelings of well-being, as in the case of believers at Laodicea (Rev. 3: 14–22). This Christless church, far from feeling any sense of desolation, was in a mood of complete satisfaction (verse 17). They depended on other resources, and because they thought they were managing so well without their Lord, they did not realize He was no longer among them.

4. The backslider who persists in his opposition to the will of God will forfeit both present and final salvation.

(a) *The Bible teaches that those who have received spiritual life can lose it, and that those once committed to Christ can leave Him.*

Jesus spoke of the possibility of His disciples becoming like salt that had lost its savour (Matt. 5: 13) or branches separated from the vine of which they had once been a part (John 15: 6). He also spoke of the ploughman who forsakes his task (Luke 9: 62) and of those who ' for a while believe, and in time of temptation fall away ' (Luke 8: 13).

Gal. 5: 4 (N.E.B.) reads:

> When you seek to be justified by the law, your relation with Christ is completely severed: you have fallen out of the domain of God's grace.

Heb. 6: 4–6 describes the judgment incurred by those who fall away after being ' made partakers of the Holy Ghost ', and after having ' tasted of the heavenly gift ' and the ' powers of the world to come ' (see also 2 Pet. 2: 20, 21; 1 Tim. 4: 1).

In the statement that God gives the believer *eternal* life the word ' eternal ' describes the *quality* of the saving life which a believer possesses only as long as he abides in Christ (see 1 John 5: 11, 12). If a man has not the Spirit of Christ he is none of His (Rom. 8: 9). Those of Christ's flock who are kept secure are they who *hear* His voice and *follow* Him (John 10: 27, 28).

Anyone who has openly repudiated the Christian faith can no longer be regarded as a saved person. This is equally true of those who completely abandon their commitments to Christian discipleship.

(*b*) *Final salvation is promised only to those who endure to the end* (Col. 1: 22, 23; Heb. 3: 14; 10: 38, 39; Jude 20, 21).

It is those who keep themselves in the love of God who are kept by Him from falling and are prepared by Him for His eternal kingdom (Jude 24).

> He that endureth to the end shall be saved (Matt. 10: 22; see also 24: 13).

> Be thou faithful unto death, and I will give thee a crown of life (Rev. 2: 10).

(*c*) *Those who do not endure to the end will be lost.*

The New Testament uses the word ' reprobate ', which means ' disapproved ', ' rejected ', ' unable and unfit to pass the test ', the equivalent of the Hebrew word of Jer. 6: 30, where the prophet spoke of those who had forsaken the Lord as ' reprobate silver . . . because the Lord hath rejected them ' (see also Rom. 1 : 28; 2 Cor. 13 : 5, 6, 7; 2 Tim. 3 : 8 and Titus 1 : 16). It is the opposite of the word translated ' approved ' as in 2 Cor. 10 : 18 and 2 Tim. 2 : 15.

Jesus declared that at the final judgment ' many ' who present themselves as having worked for Him will be banished because they are workers of iniquity (Matt. 7 : 22, 23). He spoke of God's verdict of expulsion upon the unprofitable servant (Matt. 25 : 30), as well as upon the servant guilty of betraying his trust, whom He will cut off and ' appoint him his portion with the unbelievers ' (Luke 12 : 46).

In 1 Cor. 3 : 15 Paul declared God's judgment on unworthy work and in verse 17 speaks of His judgment on the man who defiles himself—' him shall God destroy '. The Apostle declared that this could be his own fate. He who could give the triumphant testimony, ' I have fought a good fight, I have finished my course, I have kept the faith ' (2 Tim. 4 : 7), also feared lest he himself should become a castaway (1 Cor. 9 : 27).

5. The Bible warns backsliders that judgment passed will be according to light received.

(a) *The backslidings of Israel are one of the prominent themes of the Bible,* and repeated attention is drawn to the false security claimed by those who thought that their privileges would secure for them preferential treatment.

History has confirmed the words of the prophets who taught that special privilege imposes greater responsibility (see Amos 3 : 1, 2; Dan. 9 : 11, 12; Matt. 3 : 7–10; Acts 13 : 46; Rom. 10 : 21).

(b) *Jesus gave this same message to His generation* (Matt. 11 : 20–24), *and confirmed its application to His Church* (Luke 12 : 48).

(c) *In the Epistles the believers are urged to learn from the example of Israel,* with the added warning that those who have known the privilege of salvation through Christ will face severe judgment (Rom. 11 : 20, 21, R.S.V.; 1 Cor. 10 : 11, 12, R.S.V.; Heb. 2 : 2, 3; 4 : 1; 10 : 29; 12 : 25).

(d) *God shows no preferential treatment in the bestowing of His grace* (Acts 10: 34, 35, 43; Rom. 10: 12), *and certainly none in the administration of His justice* (Rom. 2: 6, 11, 12).

This latter portion (see verses 8, 9) is joined in teaching with such passages as 1 Cor. 6: 9, 10; Gal. 6: 7, 8; Eph. 5: 3–6; 2 Tim. 2: 19; 1 John 3: 7–10, to refute any idea that God will tolerate behaviour in His children which would be condemned if committed by the ungodly.

6. Backsliding injures the cause of Christ as well as the spiritual life of the backslider.

Backsliding in conduct brings open discredit to the name of Christ, and gives the ungodly occasion to deride the name and power of God (Rom. 2: 21–24; 1 Tim. 6: 1).

By turning from Christ after having experienced saving grace, the backslider bears witness against Him and His way.

7. Backsliding does not diminish the gracious fulness of the gospel message; the backslider is still within the provision of pardoning mercy.

(*a*) The declaration of the changeless grace of God given to backsliding Israel is given also to His people today (see Jer. 3: 12–14; Hos. 14: 1–4; Rev. 2: 5, 16; 3: 2, 3, 16, 18–20).

(*b*) The way of restoration is by repentance and faith. The backslider must again receive Christ as Lord and Saviour, renewing his trust in Him who pardons and reinstates the penitent.

(*c*) If, on the other hand, those things which cause separation from God are persisted in, the backslider has no prospect other than ' a certain fearful expectation of judgment ' (Heb. 10: 27, R.V.).

8. The security against backsliding is to ' walk in the Spirit '.

All backsliding arises either from neglect or refusal to heed the guidance of the Spirit. But restoration is possible and only those who have ' outraged the Spirit of grace ' (Heb. 10: 29, R.S.V.) by deliberate and continued disobedience are finally lost.

10

SANCTIFICATION

'*We believe that it is the privilege of all believers to be "wholly sanctified", and that their ".whole spirit and soul and body" may "be preserved blameless unto the coming of our Lord Jesus Christ"* (1 Thess. 5: 23)' (Article 10).

Section I. INTRODUCTION

The full quotation is

The very God of peace sanctify you wholly; and I pray God your whole spirit and soul and body be preserved blameless unto the coming of our Lord Jesus Christ. Faithful is He that calleth you, who also will do it (1 Thess. 5: 23, 24).

1. There are three aspects of this divine activity:

(a) In relation to *the work itself*—to 'sanctify you wholly'.

(b) In relation to *the completeness of its effect* which leaves no part of the personality untouched—'your whole spirit and soul and body'—that is, all the faculties through which man has relationship with God, with himself and with other men.

(c) In relation to *time*—'unto the coming of our Lord Jesus Christ'.

2. Sanctification is a divine work.

It is God who sanctifies and who preserves in sanctification.

3. Sanctification is not only the privilege of all believers but God's call to all (verse 24).

This truth is reinforced by 1 Thess. 4: 3: 'This is the *will* of God, even your sanctification', and by 2 Thess. 2: 13:

145

God hath from the beginning chosen you to salvation through sanctification of the Spirit and belief of the truth.   (See also Eph. 1: 4.)

4. The teaching that sanctification is concerned with the purpose of God that His children should be like Him in holiness and love is further illustrated by 1 Thess. 3: 12, 13:

The Lord make you to increase and abound in love one toward another, and toward all men, even as we do toward you: to the end He may stablish your hearts unblameable in holiness before God, even our Father, at the coming of our Lord Jesus Christ with all His saints.

5. These prayers which declare what God will do, appear in a context of instructions concerning what believers should do.

To adapt Phil. 2: 12, 13, believers are to work out their sanctification with fear and trembling, for it is God who works in them both to will and to do His good pleasure.

Section II.   THE NATURE OF SANCTIFICATION

1. The word ' sanctify ' means ' to make holy '.

It appears in the Bible frequently as the translation of the Hebrew and Greek words used to declare the holiness of God.

The word ' sanctification ' is used in two senses: (1) to describe the *action* by which men are made holy, and (2) to denote the *result* of this hallowing.   The first refers to sanctifying action, and the second to a sanctified state.

The words of Article 10—' to be " wholly sanctified " '— refer to the sanctified state but, because of their setting in 1 Thess. 5: 23, fully imply that this state results from the divine act.

2. All holiness has its source in the holiness of God.

All holy things are holy only because of their relationship to

Him (see chap. 3, sect. II, 4 (*a*)). Teaching about holiness in man is thus inevitably linked with teaching about the holiness of God.

(*a*) *The word ' holy ' is used to express His exalted majesty and power, His awesomeness and His separateness.*

> The high and lofty One that inhabiteth eternity, whose name is Holy ' (Isa. 57: 15).

This thought of God produced in man feelings of solemnity, reverence and dread (for example, Gen. 28: 16, 17; Exod. 3: 5, 6), making him fearful of approaching God in any other than a prescribed way. This reverence was given not only to God, but to everything which was regarded as belonging to Him in an exclusive sense—sacred places, times, ceremonies, objects and persons. All such were set apart from other uses and treated as being holy unto God.

In keeping with their holy use, all objects used in divine worship had to be as perfect as man could make them, and all animals used in sacrifice had to be without blemish.

The requirements for the priesthood were primarily the same. The priests were dedicated to God and freed from other occupations so that they could serve Him in the appointed way. They were prepared for their vocation by ritual cleansing. In this sense, their holiness was formal and external and did not necessarily refer to their inward moral character.

(*b*) *The holiness of God consists in His righteousness and moral excellence.*

> The Lord of hosts is exalted in justice, and the Holy God shows Himself holy in righteousness (Isa. 5: 16, R.S.V.).

Continuing revelation resulted in a corresponding change in defining what was meant by a ' holy ' man and a ' holy ' nation. Now the man claiming to represent God had to be freed from moral defilement; he must manifest in his inward character the righteous nature of the One whom he served (see Ps. 15 and Ps. 24: 3–6).

(*c*) *Every deepening of the revelation of the holiness of God brought with it the increasing realization that no man was worthy to stand before Him* (Ps. 130: 3, 4; 143: 2; Job 25: 4–6).

Yet side by side with this searching truth went the promise that He who dwells ' in the high and holy place ', would dwell ' with him also that is of a contrite and humble spirit, to revive the spirit of the humble, and to revive the heart of the contrite ones ' (Isa. 57: 15). (See also Isa. 1: 11–20, and 6: 1–8.)

(*d*) *In Jesus this experience was both perfected and made available for every believer.*

He is the Sacrifice, the Priest and the Man who is holy in every sense of the word. That which preceded Him was merely a symbol. Unless the symbol is seen in relation to Him, its message is incomplete and confusing.

He is the way to God and the means by whom God's holy life comes to men, and by whom all men, all places and all seasons can be set apart for God and made to manifest His glory.

3. The sanctified state has two main aspects.

Ye are the temple of the living God; as God hath said, I will dwell in them, and walk in them; and I will be their God, and they will be My people (2 Cor. 6: 16).

(*a*) Paul's words present both truths: that of *belonging to God*, of being ' set apart ', being ' separated ' unto Him and His service, as were the Temple and the priests in Old Testament times, and that of *being possessed and indwelt by God* in such a way that His holy nature is shed abroad in the life of the believer.

These two aspects introduce new words. To the thought of *being set apart for God* belong such terms as consecration, dedication, presenting oneself a living sacrifice. To the thought of *God's indwelling* and its effect belong such terms as godliness (Godlikeness), being filled with the Spirit, showing forth the fruit of the Spirit, purity of heart and perfect love.

A word which unites and fulfils both truths is ' Christlikeness ', for Jesus lived a life of complete consecration and manifested the holy love of God in human form.

Every movement toward holiness involves a movement away from its opposite.

(b) *Being separated to God* means being separated *from* every contrary commitment. No one can serve two opposing interests at the same time. This principle is illustrated in the sanctification of the Jewish Sabbath, which could be dedicated to God in the way He required only by freeing it from ' weekday ' occupations (Exod. 20: 8); and by Paul's portrayal of the Christian as an active-service soldier who is bound to keep himself free from civilian entanglements (2 Tim. 2: 3, 4).

(c) *Being holy in character* means being separate *from* all that is contrary to the divine nature; the believer must be willing to renounce all that is sinful (2 Cor. 6: 14, 17; 1 John 1: 6, 9).

Statements about sanctification, therefore, are inadequate if part is taken for the whole. It is necessary to speak both of dedication and of cleansing, of the response required from man as well as of the sanctifying work God alone can do. Briefly, sanctification involves consecration and the divine indwelling which purifies and imparts positive goodness. Such an experience is expressed concisely in Titus 2: 14, where our Saviour Jesus Christ ' gave Himself for us, that He might redeem us from all iniquity, and purify unto Himself a peculiar people, zealous of good works '. (See also Ezek. 36: 25–28.)

4. The words ' consecration ' and ' sanctification ' are used in Salvation Army teaching in a distinctive way.

(a) The words ' consecrate ' and ' dedicate ' appear in the Authorized Version of the Old Testament as alternate translations of various Hebrew words which mean ' to devote ', ' to separate ' or ' to set apart ', or ' to fill the hand ' (as with an offering). These two words do not appear in the Authorized Version of the New Testament save in Heb. 7: 28 (where ' perfected ' is a more precise translation) and in Heb. 9: 18; 10: 20 (where the original word means ' to make new ', ' to inaugurate ').

Difficulty arises when the words ' consecrate ' and ' consecration ' are used with the meaning of ' sanctify ' and ' sanctification '. Reference to the Greek text of the New Testament shows that the writer used language which meant ' to make holy '.

In Salvation Army usage the word ' consecration ' is understood to mean a dedicating act done by man, while the word
' sanctification ' is used to describe the act by which God bestows
His holiness on that which is consecrated.

(*b*) This distinction still applies in those instances where the
Bible speaks of sanctification as though it were the work of man.
In their context such references in no way contradict the truth
that sanctification is of God.

Whenever a man is described as sanctifying himself, what he
is doing is to fulfil all the needful conditions in order that God
may possess and hallow him. When, for example, Moses is
spoken of as sanctifying the tabernacle or men for the priesthood,
he is separating for God's use as holy this place of worship and
these men. But the first acceptance and hallowing was still with
God (Lev. 20: 7, 8).

(*c*) When Jesus is spoken of as being sanctified by the Father
or by Himself (John 10: 36; 17: 19), the reference is to His
mission and means that He dedicated Himself to the work the
Father had commissioned Him to do.

5. Holiness in the life of Jesus, who was ' holy, blameless, unstained, separated from sinners ' (Heb. 7: 26, R.S.V.), was the manifestation of His divine nature, while holiness in man is the outcome of a transforming work of grace.

(*a*) *The life of Jesus revealed many truths about the nature o,
holiness which otherwise would have remained hidden.*

Jesus showed that holy love can be manifested in life as man
has to live it. In particular, He revealed that a holy life can be
lived in a sinful world. He demonstrated the reaction of holiness
to the onslaught of evil. In temptation He triumphed, being ' in
all points tempted like as we are, yet without sin ' (Heb. 4: 15).
The severest testing served but to demonstrate the integrity of
His holy living.

The purpose of His life and death was not only to *display*
holiness but to *impart* it, to make it possible for sinful men to
become ' partakers of the divine nature '.

(*b*) *Holiness in men is possible only when Jesus, who once lived among men, lives in them in the transforming power of His Spirit.*

This transformation is concerned with the sanctifying work God does *in* and *through* men by:

(i) *delivering* from self and sin;

(ii) *purifying* from defilement;

(iii) *transforming* their lives in holy love so that devotion to God takes the place of devotion to self, and wrong-doing is replaced by holy conduct.

Bible statements concerning sanctification speak of this three-fold change with varied emphasis, so that it is important always to consider all such texts in association with each other.

The heart of the experience is well expressed by the words of Paul:

> I have been crucified with Christ; it is no longer I who live, but Christ who lives in me; and the life I now live in the flesh I live by faith in the Son of God, who loved me and gave Himself for me (Gal. 2: 20, R.S.V.).

In other words, holiness in man is the moral quality of character and conduct shown by those who, through the in-dwelling Spirit, share Christ's nature and consent to be ruled by Him.

Section III. GOD'S PROVISION FOR SANCTIFICATION

1. The Atonement provides for man's sanctification as well as His salvation.

> Jesus . . . that He might sanctify the people with His own blood, suffered without the gate (Heb. 13: 12).

(See also Rom. 8: 3, 4; Eph. 5: 25–27; 1 Pet. 2: 21, 24; 1 John 3: 5, 8.)

(*a*) *This means that the work of Christ*, ' who of God is made unto us wisdom, and righteousness, and sanctification, and redemption' (1 Cor. 1: 30), *provides the possibility of being sanctified in Christ quite as much as being justified in Christ.*

Sanctification, justification, regeneration and adoption are equally part of the inheritance of those who trust in the saving virtue of the Atonement. All are blessings of the New Covenant, which the Epistle to the Hebrews likens to a legacy that Jesus has bequeathed to His heirs (Heb. 9: 15–17).

(*b*) In accord with this aspect of doctrine, *the New Testament speaks in a number of places of the provision whereby every believer can be sanctified, with all the privileges and obligations this inheritance brings:*

> Our old man is crucified with Him, that the body of sin might be destroyed, that henceforth we should not serve sin (Rom. 6: 6).
>
> Our lower nature has no claim upon us; we are not obliged to live on that level (Rom. 8: 12, N.E.B.).
>
> You have put off the old nature with its practices and have put on the new nature, which is being renewed in knowledge after the image of its Creator (Col. 3: 9, 10, R.S.V.).

(See also 1 Cor. 1: 2; 3: 22, 23; 6: 11; Eph. 1: 3; 2: 6; Col. 3: 3; Heb. 10: 10, 12–14; 1 Pet. 2: 9.)

(*c*) *This means that God's provision for man's sanctification is complete.* Whenever this work of grace is not being fully expressed in a Christian's life, the explanation lies not in the lack of divine provision but in his failure to make co-operating response.

(*d*) *In the purpose, calling and provision of God all can be holy people.*

Romans 6, Ephesians 4–6, Colossians 3 and 4, the First Epistle of Peter and the First Epistle of John are concerned with the teaching that union with Christ has invested every Christian with the most exalted *privilege*, and at the same time has placed upon him the solemn *obligation* to see that his manner of life is in accord with the dignity and resources of this inheritance.

These Scriptures show that if a Christian is not living in the realization of the sanctifying blessings of which they speak, it is because, through lack of knowledge, faith or willingness, he is not claiming what God *has* provided.

Likewise, the *obligations* set forth are binding upon *all*, without exception. Underlying these exhortations is the basic truth that committal to Christ as Saviour means committal to His total purpose in salvation. No one can have just as much of Jesus Christ as he may choose and no more, or accept the privileges of salvation without the obligations.

Thus it should be seen that Bible teaching about the power and purpose of the Atonement firmly establishes and constantly applies the truth that it is the privilege and the obligation of all believers to be wholly sanctified.

2. The transformation that sanctification requires and provides is effected by the indwelling Spirit of God.

(*a*) *The indwelling of the Holy Spirit as the outcome of the Atonement is the greatest blessing that men receive*, for on His presence and action depends the imparting of all other graces of salvation.

He, who is of one essence with the Father and the Son, communicates the presence of the Triune God, so that they who have the Spirit, have the Spirit of Christ and the means by which they may be ' filled with all the fulness of God ' (Eph. 3: 16–19). With this privilege comes the corresponding obligation to be responsive in will and act to all the Spirit's ministry.

(*b*) *In relation to sanctification, the Holy Spirit brings the life and power that makes holiness possible, while a wholehearted response to all the Spirit imparts makes holiness actual* (see Rom. 8: 1–17).

These Scriptures show that the Holy Spirit operates not only as the source from which all goodness flows—

> The fruit of the Spirit is love, joy, peace, longsuffering, gentleness, goodness, faith, meekness, temperance: against such there is no law (Gal. 5: 22, 23)—

but as the mighty opponent of all that is evil—

> The flesh lusteth against the Spirit, and the Spirit against the flesh: and these are contrary the one to the other (Gal. 5: 17).

The exposition in chap. 6, sect. IX, 2 (*a*) of the term,

' the flesh ', shows that these verses of Romans and Galatians refer to the Holy Spirit's conflict with the root cause of man's spiritual weakness.

Man's spiritual need lies not only in his lack of positive goodness, but in his bondage to a sinful principle which frustrates every effort he makes toward moral reformation. Thus it is necessary to speak of:

> (i) a work of *liberation*, by which man is delivered from bondage to sin and enabled to live a Spirit-directed life;
>
> (ii) a work of *illumination and persuasion*, in which the Holy Spirit makes plain the purposes and promises of God, and the responding commitments that man should make;
>
> (iii) a work of *purification and transformation*, which is involved in and flows from new relationship. This enables man to become a partaker of the divine nature and to manifest the graces of godliness.

Sanctification is thus effected in the lives of those willing that this liberating, purifying and transforming work should be done within them, and who express their willingness by corresponding trust and dedication.

Section IV.   THE NATURE OF THE RESPONSE GOD REQUIRES

1. The call to holiness is a call to all believers to live in continual fellowship with the risen Saviour.

(*a*) This teaching is referred to in Gal. 5: 24—' They that are Christ's have crucified the flesh with the affections and lusts '— and is the basis of all that is said in Romans, chap. 6.

> Reckon ye also yourselves to be dead indeed unto sin, but alive unto God through Jesus Christ our Lord (Rom. 6: 11).

Believers must do more than associate themselves with Calvary as those who look upon the Sin-bearer who suffers there *for* them. They are called to identify themselves with Him *on* the Cross, as being crucified *with* Him and fully united with Him, and He with them, so that His death means the death of their old nature, leading to a new life in the power of the Resurrection (2 Cor. 5: 14, 15; Col. 3: 3).

It is this identification with the Lord Jesus Christ in the power and purpose of His death, and of His life risen from the dead, that brings the liberation, purification and transformation spoken of in sect. III, 2 (*b*). On the one hand holiness is separation from a life of sin and failure and, on the other, it is a life possessed by God's transforming grace (Rom. 6: 4, 6).

(*b*) *Man cannot be holy unless he is delivered from sin.*

Sin is not only the power which moves men to do evil things; it is the cause of the moral corruption that invades the hearts and minds of those who commit the sins (see Mark 7: 15, 21–23). Paul wrote of ' the carnal mind ' which is ' enmity against God: for it is not subject to the law of God, neither indeed can be ' (Rom. 8: 7), and of ' the flesh ' which ' lusteth against the spirit ' (Gal. 5: 17). The holy purpose of God cannot be fulfilled in a life affected in this way. ' The temple ' must be cleansed from defilement and separated from that which defiles (see 1 Cor. 3: 17).

(*c*) *There is one means of deliverance—that provided by the Atonement.*

The announcement of the gospel is that God wills and has made it possible for men to be set free from sin. The Risen Saviour is the supreme antagonist and conqueror of sin (see Rom. 6: 1–11).

(*d*) This work of grace involves more than a deliverance from sin; *its power and its purpose penetrate to the depths of personality and leave no part of life untouched.*

In this life-through-death transformation, all the past with its sin, self-will and self-dependence is left behind.

Phil. 3: 3–11 and related Scriptures show that Paul's committal to Christ—to know Him in the power of His resurrection and to be made ' conformable unto His death '—meant far more than a deliverance from sin. The totality of his life lived apart from Christ, with all its thinking and acting, with the things he had valued as well as those he had deplored, was left on the other side of the Cross.

Because Christ claims men for God, He condemned ' sin in the flesh ' and everything in man that opposes this claim. It is both in the power and purpose of His death and in the power and endowment of His risen life that He plants His separating Cross between the life lived ' according to the flesh ' and the life lived ' according to the Spirit '. The man who thus knows death and life in Christ is blessed, not only by being released from all ungodliness, but by being united to the divine resources which make it possible to put on the new man, ' created after the likeness of God in true righteousness and holiness ' (Eph. 4: 24, R.S.V.).

The total nature of this separation becomes still more apparent when it is realized that those united to the Risen Lord share His ascended life (Eph. 2: 4, 6; Col. 3: 1–3).

2. The revelation that God wills and in Christ has provided the means for His people's sanctification, includes the call to them to make a response of faith and consecration.

(a) *In this setting the word consecration includes the acceptance of the implications of living a holy life.*

This act of faith and consecration expresses man's trust in God's sanctifying power, and his own willingness to be sanctified.

Examples of this call to consecration are found in Rom. 12: 1, 2; 1 Cor. 6: 19, 20; 2 Cor. 6: 16, 17; 7: 1; 1 Pet. 1: 14, 15; 1 John 3: 2, 3.

These Scriptures show that as an accompaniment and expression of sanctifying faith there must be:

>   (i) an act of committal to God which involves the giving of oneself fully to Him;
>   (ii) the working out of the implications of this committal in every department of life.

(b) *The teaching concerning sanctifying faith and consecration is closely related to the teaching about repentance and faith, which are the responses necessary to the receiving of salvation* (see chap. 8, sect. I, para. 2).

The requirement of holiness is that Christ is both fully received and fully expressed. The faith of those who fulfil this requirement is marked by dependence and dedication. In utter dependence on God, the heart is opened to receive the work of grace He alone can do, and the whole life is dedicated to show forth the effect of this divine action.

(*c*) *Sanctifying faith can be described in the same language as saving faith. It is that act of personal heart trust by which the seeker commits himself to God and accepts as his own the sanctification which God so freely offers* (see chap. 8, sect. III, para. 1 (*c*)).

The believing seeker looks to the same Saviour and kneels at the same Cross. He is inspired by the same act of Atonement, by the divine will and love it expresses, and by the grace and blessing that flow from it.

The Lord Jesus Christ, who was received as *justifying* Saviour, is now received as *sanctifying* Saviour (1 Cor. 6: 11), as He who ' of God is made unto us . . . sanctification ' (1 Cor. 1: 30).

Sanctifying faith also recognizes that the working of God is according to His infinite nature, thus transcending the bounds of human consciousness.

(*d*) *Consecration is also akin to repentance in that it has a positive and a negative aspect, a turning to God in submission and obedience, and a turning from all that is against Him.*

All acts of consecration involve acts of renunciation. Holiness is marked by what is removed from the life as well as by what is received. Thus every direction to ' put on ' godly character and conduct is balanced by exhortation to ' put off ' all that is ungodly. The positive dominates and calls forth the acts of renunciation. All denials of self and sin co-exist with a corresponding ' Yes ' to God and righteousness.

To the comprehensive question, ' What, then, has to be renounced? ' the answer is, 'All that cannot be consecrated to God '. Being wholly dedicated to God does not mean that there cannot be other dedications in life, but these are to be subordinate to this main devotion.

Christ's law demands that family, business, social and bodily obligations must be faithfully discharged as part of the whole offering (see 1 Cor. 10: 31; Col. 3: 17, 23). In Romans, chapters 12 and 13, Paul commences with the call to holy consecration, then proceeds to speak of other dedications (service to the Church, to all men, to the State and so on), showing these to be a necessary part of the offering to God and how they are to be fulfilled in harmony with it.

(e) *Consecration to holiness includes dedication*:

(i) *To be God's temple or dwelling place.* This calls for a heart open to receive Him and the preserving of body, soul and spirit from defilement (1 Cor. 6: 17–20).

(ii) *To be His servant*, giving the whole being, with its possibilities and possessions, to live and serve as He disposes and directs. This involves the abandoning of any self-ownership which might arise in opposition to this dedication (as in Luke 9: 23, 24; 2 Cor. 5: 15) and of all compromise with iniquity (as in 2 Tim. 2: 20–26).

(iii) *To holiness of conduct.* The root demand for dedication to righteousness, with its corresponding denial of any place being given to sinful indulgence, is presented in Rom. 6: 13 and its context. Christ's followers are to say an unqualified ' No ' to every action unworthy of His name (2 Tim. 2: 19), and conversely they are to commend their Master by right conduct (see Matt. 5: 16; 1 Pet. 2: 12).

(iv) *To holy character.* Holiness is inward as well as outward. In 2 Cor. 7: 1 Paul wrote of cleansing oneself from all filthiness of the spirit, as well as from all filthiness of the flesh, while the Scriptures which deal so fully with what is to be ' put off ' and ' put on ' (as in Ephesians, chapters 4, 5, 6; Colossians, chapters 3, 4) speak of an inward condition of heart as well as of outward actions.

(v) *To holy influence.* Response to the divine call to holiness is not confined to concern for oneself; the gospel presents God as willing the sanctification of all His people. Thus all who believe and obey are committed to repudiate all influences that would work against this greater purpose and to cultivate every means that would serve it (see Eph. 4: 1–16).

(*f*) *The standard by which all these requirements are measured is not left in uncertainty; it is the standard of Christlikeness.*

Christ Himself is set forth as an example—John 13: 15; Rom. 15: 5; 1 Pet. 2: 21; 1 John 4: 17.

There is a call

(i) to have the mind of Christ inspiring both concern for others (Phil. 2: 1–15) and a renunciation of sin (1 Pet. 4: 1, 2);

(ii) to ' walk in the light, as He is in the light ' (1 John 1: 7);

(iii) to purify oneself ' as He is pure ' (1 John 3: 3);

(iv) to receive one another, ' as Christ also received us ' (Rom. 15: 7);

(v) to ' walk in love, as Christ also hath loved us ' (Eph. 5: 2);

(vi) to manifest to others the forgiveness received through Him (Eph. 4: 32) and from Him (Col. 3: 13);

(vii) to ' walk, even as He walked ' (1 John 2: 6).

3. The experience of holiness involves both a crisis and a process—the initial dedication when the commitment is made, and the process or subsequent action by which the implications of this commitment are worked out in every department of life.

(*a*) *This continued action affects character and conduct in both a negative and a positive way,* as shown in 2 Cor. 7: 1:

Let us cleanse ourselves from all filthiness of the flesh and spirit, perfecting holiness in the fear of God.

This purifying of the life is presented in death and life terms:

(i) *Negatively*:

Mortify ['put to death' R.S.V., N.E.B.] the deeds of the body (Rom. 8: 13).

Your life is hid with Christ in God. . . . Put to death therefore what is earthly in you (Col. 3: 3, 5, R.S.V.).

(ii) *Negatively and positively*:

Let us therefore cast off the works of darkness, and let us put on the armour of light. Let us walk honestly, as in the day; not in rioting and drunkenness, not in chambering and wantonness, not in strife and envying. But put ye on the Lord Jesus Christ, and make not provision for the flesh, to fulfil the lusts thereof (Rom. 13: 12–14).

This is a putting to death by *ceasing to make any ' provision '* for such interests, giving them no place in imagination, consideration or action. Such denial of all willed attention to things which defile is the only way in which Rom. 6: 11 can be fulfilled in practice. It is the necessary attitude of one who, in obedience to Col. 3: 1, 2, *is making every ' provision '* for godly living. Patterns of conduct which belong to the old life are put off, and not carried over into the new.

By these commands to ' mortify the flesh ', Christians are not being called upon to copy the practice of those who seek by acts of rigorous self-effort to exorcize evil from their being. They are called upon, however, on the one hand to discard and constantly to bar those things which Christ has condemned (Rom. 8: 3) and, on the other, continually to receive and express the new nature He imparts.

(*b*) *The fulfilling of this commitment requires also that all the affections and motives of the heart, as well as outward conduct, are to be submitted to the transforming purpose and power of the indwelling Spirit.*

It is thus the duty of the sanctified to cultivate the Christian graces they receive from God. This is a necessary part of their dedication to holy character (see para. 2 (*e*) iv).

These exhortations do not diminish in any way the doctrine that these graces have their origin in God; nor does the truth that they are God's gift cancel the need for a man so to co-operate that these graces will have full expression in his life. For example, the first chapter of 2 Peter sets forth with equal prominence both aspects of this teaching:

> (i) It is ' Jesus our Lord ' whose ' divine power hath given unto us all things which pertain to life and godliness ' and the ' exceeding great and precious promises ' by which men may become ' partakers of the divine nature ' (verses 2–4).
>
> (ii) It is the duty of Christians to cultivate and express the distinctive qualities of the divine nature our Lord bestows (verses 5–11).

This rule applies supremely to the grace of love. The Scriptures show that the only source of the loving nature is God Himself. They speak of love as a spiritual gift to be sought above all others (1 Cor. 13), as a ' fruit of the Spirit ' (Gal. 5: 22), and as being ' shed abroad in our hearts by the Holy Ghost which is given to us ' (Rom. 5: 5). Yet love is spoken of in terms of command, as well as in terms of a gift to be received. There is constant repetition of the command to live lovingly.

Jesus spoke of the command to be loving as being the greatest commandment of all (Matt. 22: 36–40), and as His paramount command to His disciples (John 13: 34, 35). (See also Rom. 12: 9, 10; 13: 8–10; 1 Cor. 16: 14; Gal. 5: 13, 14, 26; Eph. 4: 15; 5: 2; Col. 3: 12–14 and 1 Thess. 4: 9.)

Love is not to be regarded primarily or exclusively as involving an emotional change. Love is real only to the extent that the whole being and all of life's encounters are subjected to its influence. No one can comply with Christ's command to be loving until he gives heart and will to receive this Christian grace and is prepared to express it in his every life situation.

Each disciple meets human attitudes which can provoke withdrawal, resentment, retaliation and similar unchristlike behaviour.

These conditions mark the way the Master went and the pathway of His followers but provide the setting in which love is specially needed and in which its undefeatable nature can be displayed. Hence the attention given to putting off unconcern, bitterness, self-assertion, enmity, strife and the like, and to putting on concern for others, helpfulness and forbearance. (See, for instance, Rom. 12: 17–21; 1 Cor. 13: 4–7; Eph. 4: 31, 32; Col. 3: 12–14; 1 John 3: 16–18.)

4. Prominence is given in the teaching of sanctification to the transforming power of the grace of love. This ' love that issues from a pure heart and a good conscience and sincere faith ' (1 Tim. 1: 5, R.S.V.) is a most important aspect of the experience and leads to the description of sanctification as the blessing of perfect love (1 John 4: 7–21).

Reasons for this prominence are:

(a) *When a man loves his neighbour with the love the Spirit imparts, he fulfils on the highest level and to the fullest degree the law of God concerning his relationship with his fellow man* (Gal. 5: 14).

> (i) He commits no sin of wilful injury against any other person, his property or reputation (Rom. 13: 10).
>
> (ii) He acts with helpfulness and concern toward his fellow man's wellbeing, as in Matt. 7: 12.
>
> (iii) He seeks to do the right thing for the right reason in the right way.

(b) *By acting in love to God and to his fellow man, a man finds release and fulfilment in his own person.*

Nothing he does is so integrating and outgoing; nothing so intensely engages the whole personality; nothing is done more freely and worthily than that which is controlled by the love of God shed abroad in the human heart.

(c) *To be controlled by the love of God is the way in which man can be like God, not in power or authority but in character* (Matt. 5: 43-48). *In no greater way can he be affected by the grace of God.*

This love born of love is directed to both God and man.

(i) *To God*, with desire to be with Him, to please Him, to serve Him and to be like Him; with a response of utter trustfulness in His unfailing graciousness to the undeserving. It is a ' perfect love ' which ' casteth out fear ' (1 John 4: 18).

(ii) *To man*, because all men are seen to be within the purpose and power of this love (2 Cor. 5: 14).

5. Sanctification is spoken of as full salvation for two main reasons:

(*a*) *Because of the comprehensiveness and thoroughness of this work of grace.*

Teaching about the comprehensive and thorough nature of sanctification has been given throughout this chapter. See, for instance: sect. I, para. 1; sect. II, para. 5 (*b*).

(*b*) *Because the sanctified man is fully surrendered to God as Lord and Saviour, and fully receptive to the sanctifying grace the Spirit continuously imparts.*

Sanctification is not a state in which there is no possibility of further advance, but one in which the obstacles to spiritual growth have been removed.

The receiving of sanctification means that what has been incomplete or inconsistent in the soul's response to God's revealed will is now put right. The removing of evils and hindrances from the heart makes growth in grace more certain and rapid than otherwise it would be.

Thus sanctification is purity, but not finality of Christian experience. The transformation which results from the receiving and showing forth of the divine nature provides unending possibility of continued spiritual development (2 Cor. 3: 18; 1 John 4: 12).

6. While sanctification can be described as full salvation it is not final salvation.

Some of the blessings salvation bestows are not realized in this life.

(a) *Final salvation alone will bring about the redemption of the body, when ' the Lord Jesus Christ . . . will change our lowly body to be like His glorious body* (Phil. 3: 21, R.S.V.). (See also 1 Cor. 15: 53, 54.)

This means that sanctification does not bestow infallibility or freedom from mistaken judgment. This would require perfect knowledge, which none but God possesses. Sanctification does, however, render people less likely to err in judgment, because they have the guidance of the Holy Spirit; they acknowledge God in all their ways and He directs their paths (Jas. 1: 5; Prov. 3: 6).

Sanctification does not give freedom from bodily and mental infirmities. Many of God's choicest saints have been great sufferers. It does, however, enable God's people to glorify Him in their afflictions, and in some instances to exercise faith for deliverance from them.

Paul's statement that ' we have this treasure in earthen vessels ' (2 Cor. 4: 7) corrects two common errors: that because men are earthen vessels they cannot have the treasure, and that if men have this treasure they will cease to be earthen vessels. Neither idea is correct.

Nowhere is it stated in the Bible that the soul's connection with the body is a hindrance to its sanctification; instead, the Scriptures show that the body, with all its appetites, powers and members, is to be sanctified to God (1 Cor. 6: 20; 2 Cor. 4: 10, 11).

The scriptural promises about holiness which relate to this life can be realized in *this* life. By this very limitation the glory of the treasure is enhanced rather than diminished, for it is thereby shown ' that the transcendent power belongs to God and not to us ' (2 Cor. 4: 7, R.S.V.).

' The Spirit of Him that raised up Jesus from the dead ' indwells mortal bodies (Rom. 8: 11) so that ' though our outer nature is wasting away, our inner nature is being renewed day by day ' (2 Cor. 4: 16, R.S.V.).

A mortal condition does not prevent the child of God from living by the Spirit and according to His leadings (Rom. 8: 13;

Gal. 5: 16, 25), nor from bringing forth the fruit of love (para. 4), but it does encourage dependence upon God.

> He said unto me, My grace is sufficient for thee: for My strength is made perfect in weakness. Most gladly therefore will I rather glory in my infirmities, that the power of Christ may rest upon me (2. Cor. 12: 9).

(*b*) *While the sanctified continue in an earthly condition they will be subject to temptation.*

Although ' without sin ', Jesus was severely tempted, and the New Testament contains many references to the temptations to which all His disciples are exposed. They are taught to expect temptation but are encouraged and guided

> (i) *by provision* of the equipment they need to meet it (as in Eph. 6: 10–18),
>
> (ii) *by promise* of divine aid in resisting it (as in 1 Cor. 10: 13),
>
> (iii) *by assurance* concerning the good ends such encounter can be made to serve (1 Pet. 1: 6, 7; Jas. 1: 12).

11

THE ULTIMATE DESTINY
OF MAN

' We believe in the immortality of the soul; in the resurrection of the body; in the general judgment at the end of the world; in the eternal happiness of the righteous; and in the endless punishment of the wicked' (Article 11).

Section I.   INTRODUCTION

1. Article 11 is concerned with ultimate things.

It speaks of the end of the world, of the destiny of man in the world to come, of things that will pass and of things that will eternally remain. This is an essential part of Christian doctrine because it is only in the light of God's ultimate actions that His preceding acts can be rightly interpreted. The Scriptures upon which this Article is based show that man has a destiny beyond death, that it is for life in the world to come that he was created, and that only in that world can God's purpose for him be completely fulfilled.

2. The Bible is our only source of knowledge concerning existence and events in a future state.

The Old Testament says but little on the subject, but more is to be found in the teaching of Christ and of His apostles. Although this makes no attempt to satisfy mere curiosity, and many questions must therefore remain unanswered until the veil is withdrawn which now hides the unseen, sufficient is revealed for man's guidance, encouragement and warning.

3. There is a sense in which these ultimate acts of the unchanging God are already operative.

(*a*) *Those who are in Christ experience a deliverance from this present evil world now, and taste the powers of the world to come* (Gal. 1: 4; Heb. 6: 5).

The Lord with whom they will eternally dwell is already with them in the fulness of His power. They are ' sealed with the promised Holy Spirit, which is the guarantee of our inheritance until we acquire possession of it ' (Eph. 1: 13, 14, R.S.V.). While still in the flesh they have an experience of resurrection power and of the heavenly life (John 5: 24; 11: 25, 26; Eph. 2: 6; Phil. 3: 20; Col. 3: 3; 2 Cor. 4: 16).

(*b*) *There is also a sense in which men already encounter the judgment of God and know something of the separation from Him which rejection of Christ brings* (John 3: 18, 36; 12: 31).

(*c*) *The end of this age will not mean the passing away of all that now is.* Temporal things will be removed, but ' those things which cannot be shaken ' will abide (2 Cor. 4: 18; Heb. 12: 26–29).

4. Bible teaching about man's ultimate destiny should be viewed and used in the light of the purpose for which it was given.

Although this teaching is concerned with God's dealings with man in the life to come, it is given to meet not his need in a future realm but in that of the present.

The purpose of this revelation is to help him commit himself to Christ as Saviour. The value of what is said about the life to come is determined by its effectiveness in constraining men to live in the light of eternity. All investigations and speculations which make no contribution to this purpose, and which are not pursued for this reason, can be set aside without loss.

Section II. LIFE AFTER DEATH

1. Death is not the end of human existence.

(a) *Death is the separation of the spirit from the body* (2 Cor. 5: 8).

The body falls into decay, while the life of the spirit continues freed from physical fetters and independent of physical manifestation.

(b) *The clearest testimony to this truth is given by Christian revelation.*

Throughout history men have had instinctive convictions that death is not the end. This conviction has been strengthened for all who feel that life must have meaning and that moral principles must have vindication. Christian revelation confirms these instinctive feelings, and discloses to every man his relation to God, to the unseen world and to eternity.

Jesus has ' brought life and immortality to light through the gospel ' (2 Tim. 1: 10) and by insistence upon this truth gave

  (i) *warning to the sinner* (Mark 8: 36, 37; Luke 12: 13–21);

  (ii) *comfort to the dying* (Luke 23: 43);

  (iii) *consolation for His followers* (John 14: 1–3; Matt. 5: 11, 12; 10: 28; John 11: 25, 26);

  (iv) *exhortations to godly living* (Luke 18: 29, 30; Mark 13: 32–37; Matt. 25: 14–30).

The importance of man's life after death is also basic to the doctrine of redemption. Jesus went to the Cross concerned about man's eternal as well as his temporal welfare (John 3: 14–16; 6: 48–51).

2. The Bible says nothing about salvation after death, but emphasizes the peril of dying in sin (John 8: 21).

It is clear that after death the individual retains his identity, together with such mental and moral powers as conscience and memory, as is made clear by the story of the Rich Man and

Lazarus (Luke 16: 19–31) and the references to Moses and Elijah at the Transfiguration (Luke 9: 30, 31). Heb. 12: 1 also speaks of the cloud of witnesses who compass us about.

Though much that lies behind the veil is a mystery, we do know that the godly are welcomed by the Lord while the ungodly are banished from His presence.

This is a comfort to the righteous (2 Cor. 5: 8; Phil. 1: 23; Rev. 14: 13), but a solemn warning to the sinful (Matt. 25: 46).

Section III. 'THE DAY OF THE LORD'

1. The resurrection and the general judgment spoken of in Article 11 will mark the establishment by God of His everlasting Kingdom.

The Scriptures refer to this as:

' the last day ' (John 6: 39),
' the day of the Lord ' (1 Thess. 5: 2; 2 Pet. 3: 10),
' the coming of the Lord ' (Jas. 5: 7),
' the appearing of Jesus Christ ' (1 Pet. 1: 7) and
' the revelation of Jesus Christ ' (1 Pet. 1: 13).

In this setting the word ' day ' has no connection with any specific period of time, but to the day of the everlasting Kingdom when God's full glory and His ultimate purpose for all creation will be realized.

2. ' The day of the Lord ' will also be ' the day of our Lord Jesus Christ '.

(1 Cor. 1: 8; see also 2 Cor. 1: 14; Phil. 1: 6, 10; 2: 16.)

Christ, who came into the world in the form of a servant (Phil. 2: 7), will be manifested in the glory of His ascended majesty and the triumphant completion of His work as Lord and Saviour (Mark 8: 38; 1 John 3: 2).

3. It will be a ' day of redemption '.

(Eph. 4: 30; see also Heb. 9: 27, 28, N.E.B.)

4. It will be a day of judgment.

(John 5: 28, 29.)

This will be the day when God ' will judge the world in righteousness by that man which He hath ordained ' (Acts 17: 31), ' when God shall judge the secrets of men by Jesus Christ ' (Rom. 2: 16). The Son to whom all judgment is given (John 5: 22) ' shall judge the quick and the dead at His appearing and His Kingdom ' (2 Tim. 4: 1).

5. It will be a day of triumph and transformation.

The Lord Jesus Christ will manifest His universal power. His enemies will become His footstool (Heb. 10: 13), and nothing out of harmony with the will of God will again be able to injure His Kingdom.

When all things in heaven and on earth are gathered together in Christ (Eph. 1: 10; Col. 1: 20), this state of things to come can be described only in the language of Scripture itself (2 Pet. 3: 13; Ps. 102: 25–27; Heb. 1: 10–12; Mark 13: 31; 1 Cor. 15: 24, 25, 28).

6. Many Bible predictions related to the time of Christ's coming, and the exact events that will mark such an occasion, are open to different interpretations.

Between these differing views The Salvation Army does not undertake to decide, but directs attention to the certainties of Christian doctrine as they affect life and conduct.

Therefore the matters of chief concern are that men should live

(a) *in hope and expectancy*, in the certainty of Christ's ultimate triumph (Phil. 2: 9–11; Rev. 11: 15);

(b) *in holiness*, receiving and expressing the life He now imparts and fulfilling the mission He appoints;

(c) *in watchfulness*, in order continually to be responsive to the challenge presented by His coming (Luke 12: 35–40; Rom. 14: 7–13; Titus 2: 12–14; 2 Pet. 3: 14; 1 John 2: 28).

Section IV. THE RESURRECTION OF THE BODY

1. This applies to all mankind.

(John 5: 25–29; Rom. 14: 9.)

2. The resurrection of the body is more than a reversal of the act of death.

The resurrection body is a form of existence adapted to the state of the world to come. A ' spiritual body ' takes the place of the ' natural body '; corruptible puts on incorruption and mortal immortality (1 Cor. 15: 42–44, 52–54).

This distinction is illustrated in the life of Jesus. He called back to life the daughter of Jairus, the son of the widow of Nain, and Lazarus of Bethany. But these three came back to the manner of life they had left and, in process of time, died again.

The resurrection of Jesus was of a different quality. By His act of calling men back to life He demonstrated that the realm of death was subject to His authority. By His own resurrection He attacked the power that death has over every man, and came forth as conqueror to an endless life (Rom. 6: 9).

It is in this sense that He is ' the firstfruits of them that slept ' (1 Cor. 15: 20) and ' the firstborn from the dead ' (Col. 1: 18). It is *His* resurrection that has become the pledge of man's resurrection, and *His* risen form the pattern of man's risen state.

3. The New Testament speaks of the blessedness of the resurrection of those who are united to Christ as Saviour.

Their triumph will be not only over death but over sin and all its effects. Their whole being will be transformed into the likeness of Christ, ' the firstborn amongst many brethren ' (Rom. 8: 29, 30; 2 Cor. 4: 16, 17; 5: 4, 5; Phil. 3: 10, 11, 20, 21), and this will be the full manifestation of the resurrection life they will enjoy (John 11: 25, 26; Rom. 8: 10, 11; Eph. 1: 19, 20).

Section V.   THE GENERAL JUDGMENT AT THE END OF THE WORLD

It is appointed unto man once to die, but after this the judgment (Heb. 9: 27).

1. The day of judgment will be one of revelation and reckoning.

The day of judgment will be one of *revelation* when the truth concerning all things will be disclosed and when judgment will be passed in the light of this revelation (1 Cor. 3: 13).

In that day of light, men will not only be confronted with the truth about themselves, but also with the truth about the purposes and power of God Himself.

2. This solemn event and its outcome is anticipated and referred to in many places in the Scriptures.

References are found in the teachings of Jesus (for example, Matt. 13: 40–43, 47–50; 16: 27; 25: 31, 32; Luke 13: 24–30); in the teaching of Peter (Acts 10: 42), Paul (Acts 17: 31), Jude (14, 15) and John (Rev. 20: 12, 13; 22: 12).

Throughout the Bible man is presented as being always exposed to the judgment of God, who searches the mind and tries the heart ' to give to every man according to his ways, according to the fruit of his doings ' (Jer. 17: 10, R.S.V.). Passages such as those found in Matt. 24, Mark 13 and Luke 21 apply to God's acts of judgment in history as well as to the final judgment, which will provide the explanation of all the judgments which have preceded it.

3. The judgments of God are not confined to final reward and condemnation only.

As the Judge of the oppressed, the fatherless, the widow and the righteous (Ps. 10: 18; 68: 5; Luke 18: 7, 8), God acts in their defence and gives comfort and reward.   In this sense God is the

One who puts wrongs right. He has both the purpose and the power to deliver, correct and restore the situations He judges, as in Exod. 6: 6 and Ps. 9 (see also Isa. 11).

All aspects of divine judgment will be seen at the general judgment.

4. The Lord Jesus Christ will be the Judge.

(See sect. III, para. 4.)

This will be His appointed office because, as man, He has fully shared our human nature and, as God, possesses the omniscience which is an attribute of the divine nature (John 5: 22; Matt. 25: 31, 32).

5. Christ will be seen ' as He is '.

(1 John 3: 2.)

This means not only that He will be seen but He will be seen in His full glory. As Lord of creation, of history, of righteousness, and of salvation, He will receive the acknowledgment spoken of in Phil. 2: 10, 11; Rev. 1: 5, 6; 5: 9, 10, 12, 13.

6. Men will learn the truth about themselves.

On the day of judgment ' God shall judge the secrets of men by Jesus Christ ' (Rom. 2: 16), who ' will bring to light the hidden things of darkness, and will make manifest the counsels of the hearts ' (1 Cor. 4: 5).

(a) *Men will see themselves as God sees them, that is, with full knowledge of all the facts.*

This ensures that the divine judgment is a righteous judgment and means that the measure of each person's light and opportunity will be taken into account (Matt. 11: 21–24; Luke 12: 48).

(b) *The value of all human actions will be revealed.* All actions will be seen in the light of

(i) *their eternal value* (1 Cor. 3: 13);

(ii) *their final effect.* Only at the end of time will the full effect of all actions be seen, whether for good or ill.

(c) *All who have heard of Jesus Christ will be judged in the light of this greater privilege and responsibility* (John 12: 48; Luke 12: 8, 9).

(d) *Men will be judged according to their deeds* (2 Cor. 5: 10; see also Matt. 16: 27; Rom. 2: 6–9; Rev. 22: 12).

(e) *This judgment will take into account sins of omission as well as commission.* Men will be held accountable for what they have failed to do (Matt. 25: 24–30).

Section VI. THE ETERNAL HAPPINESS OF THE RIGHTEOUS

1. The eternal happiness of the righteous lies in the fact that

(a) *they are forever with God, in whose presence there is fulness of joy* (1 Thess. 4: 17; Ps. 16: 11);

(b) *their whole being is fully in accord with their heavenly surroundings*; and

(c) *they rejoice in the redeeming grace that has brought them into the divine presence and fitted them to be there* (John 14: 3; Rev. 5: 9, 10).

The righteous are those who 'have washed their robes, and made them white in the blood of the Lamb' (Rev. 7: 14).

2. The word 'heaven' is used in the Bible in at least two distinct senses.

(a) *'Heaven' is used to indicate the space beyond the earth.*

The word is used in this sense in Gen. 1: 1—' In the beginning God created the heaven and the earth '.

This is the heaven and the earth that will pass away (Matt. 24: 35; 2 Pet. 3: 7, 10; Rev. 6: 14), to be replaced by a new heaven and a new earth (2 Pet. 3: 13; Rev. 21: 1).

(b) *The word ' heaven ' is used also to define the eternal dwelling place of God, and the destined abode of His redeemed children.*

Jesus spoke of the Father ' which is in heaven ' (Matt. 5: 16; 6: 9; 16: 17; 23: 9), and of Himself as having ' come from heaven ' (John 3: 12, 13; 6: 33, 38, 42).

Jesus spoke of heaven as being the eternal home of God's children (Matt. 5: 12; 6: 20), ' My Father's house ' (John 14: 2) and ' the Kingdom prepared for you from the foundation of the world ' (Matt. 25: 34).

New Testament writers refer to the ascended Lord Jesus as being in heaven (Eph. 6: 9; Col. 4: 1; Heb. 9: 24; 1 Pet. 3: 22), and this heavenly abode is also described as ' the presence of His glory ' (Jude 24) and ' a better country ' (Heb. 11: 16).

When heaven is thought of as a *place*, it should be in the light of such Scriptures as 1 Cor. 15: 24, that is, as an expression of the triumph of the Kingdom of God (see sect. III, para. 5).

3. The future state of the redeemed will be one of supreme blessedness.

I reckon that the sufferings of this present time are not worthy to be compared with the glory which shall be revealed in us (Rom. 8: 18).

The Bible speaks, for example, of the throne of God, the sea of glass, gates of pearl, God's glory lighting up the whole place, the river of the water of life, the tree of life, music and singing. Such language is figurative and represents spiritual realities surpassing our highest imagination. The inspired writers used material figures to convey the highest possible conception of the blessedness of heaven; and the reality is always greater than the symbol.

4. Life in heaven will abound in joy because:

(a) *The Kingdom of God will be manifested in its full glory, freed from all impurities and imperfections* (Rev. 21: 4, 5; 7: 16; 22: 3; 21: 27).

(b) The full purpose of God's redeeming grace will be fulfilled.

God will be fully known as Lord and Redeemer, and the greatest joy of the redeemed will issue from their relationship with God. Their spirits will be united with His Spirit and will manifest the transformation which results from this communion (Phil. 3: 20, 21, R.S.V.; 1 John 3: 2; John 17: 23, 24).

(c) Men will be fulfilling the purpose for which they were created.

Jesus described the redeemed as being welcomed into ' the Kingdom prepared for you from the foundation of the world ' (Matt. 25: 34). They will be engaged in the noblest employment as together they ' serve Him day and night in His temple ' (Rev. 7: 15).

(d) This destined home is a place of growth and progress.

Heaven is a Kingdom of infinite possibilities. By the parables of the Talents (Matt. 25: 14–30) and the Pounds (Luke 19: 11–27), Jesus taught that the faithful servant is given opportunity to direct to greater tasks the increased powers he has developed by work well done.

(e) The joys of heaven are eternally secure.

It is ' an inheritance incorruptible, and undefiled, and that fadeth not away ' (1 Pet. 1: 4).

Section VII. THE ENDLESS PUNISHMENT OF THE WICKED

1. The endless punishment of the wicked is that they are banished from the presence of God.

The words ' everlasting punishment ' are found in Matt. 25: 46—' These shall go away into everlasting punishment '—and it is in the teaching of Jesus Christ that the most solemn warnings about this state are found.

2. The suffering and loss involved in this separation is spoken of in many ways.

Again the language is largely figurative, but again the reality is greater than the symbol.

Jesus spoke of the doom of the wicked as ' outer darkness ' (Matt. 8: 12; 25: 30), ' fire that never shall be quenched ' (Mark 9: 43), and as causing ' wailing and gnashing of teeth ' (Matt. 13: 42, 50). He compared the wicked to guests shut out from the feast (Matt. 25: 10, 11), tares that are burned and worthless fish that are cast away (Matt. 13: 30, 48).

The New Testament describes this state by using words which are translated *destruction* (Matt. 7: 13; Phil. 3: 19; 2 Thess. 1: 9); *perdition* (Rev. 17: 11), which also means destruction or ruin; *to perish* (John 3: 16; 2 Thess. 2: 10; 2 Pet. 2: 12; 3: 9) and the *second death* (Rev. 2: 11; 21: 8).

The distinctive word ' *gehenna* ', in the New Testament used to describe the place of final punishment, is itself a symbolic form of speech and refers to ' the valley of Hinnom '. This valley formed the southern boundary of the city of Jerusalem and, in permanent condemnation of the idol worship which had been practised there, part of the valley (known also as Topheth) had been turned into a rubbish tip where refuse was burned. No stronger picture of rejection could be presented to the Jewish mind than the idea of being cast into *gehenna*, the place of desecration, corruption and destruction (see 2 Chron. 33: 6; 2 Kings 23: 10; Jer. 7: 31; 19: 2, 6–13; and compare Isa. 66: 24 with Mark 9: 48). This geographical allusion is saying that the most solemn realities in the life to come answer to these ideas symbolically presented.

3. Banishment from God is the most serious form of condemnation.

This is described as the ' second death ', the culmination of that separation from God which began on earth, and is the opposite of the ' life ' or ' eternal life ' that the Lord Jesus Christ imparts to those who accept Him as Saviour.

Jesus spoke of the unsaved as being in a place which is ' prepared for the devil and his angels ', in contrast to the joy of the blessed who are welcomed to heaven as being ' the kingdom prepared for you ' (Matt. 25: 41, 34).

4. The Bible contrasts the doom of the wicked with the bliss of the righteous, and speaks of both as being eternal.

In the New Testament the same Greek word '*aiōnios*', translated in the Authorized Version sometimes by the word ' eternal ' and sometimes by the word ' everlasting ', as in John 3: 15, 16, is used on the one hand to describe God (Rom. 16: 26), the Kingdom of the Lord Jesus Christ (2 Pet. 1: 11), salvation (Heb. 5: 9), redemption (Heb. 9: 12), the inheritance of the saints (Heb. 9: 15), and the new life they receive by redemption (over forty instances); and on the other hand to describe the fire of *gehenna* (Matt. 25: 41), the punishment of the rejected (Matt. 25: 46), and their ' destruction from the presence of the Lord, and from the glory of His power ' (2 Thess. 1: 9). Similarly Dan. 12: 2 contrasts everlasting life with everlasting contempt.

The word ' *aiōnios* ' has therefore a twofold meaning—that of unending duration (something that is age-long or everlasting), and that which belongs to the age to come, that is, possessing a quality different from that of the things of time. Both meanings are present when this word is applied to the life to come. Thus while eternal fire and eternal judgment refer to a judgment which belongs to the coming age, the use of the word ' eternal ' carries also the meaning of endlessness.

In relation to the enduring nature of final banishment from God, some have held that the wicked will be annihilated, blotted out of existence. In support of this idea they take such terms as 'death ', ' destruction ' and ' perishing ' to mean cessation of existence, but the New Testament does not so use these terms in reference to the future state of the wicked.

Others look for a hope of their eventual release, but can do so only by setting aside Bible declarations to the contrary.

5. The final state of the wicked has been determined by their own choice.

(*a*) *This is the final outcome of their resistance to all godly influences that would have turned them from the error of their ways.*

The finally impenitent go where their heart is—with those who do not want God and His way.

(*b*) *Men go to hell in direct opposition to God's will and to His loving purpose to save and change them.*

He created men to live in fellowship with Him and to be like Him.

At utmost cost He acted to save men from sin and its consequences, and to bring them to Himself (John 3: 16; 1 John 4: 14).

(*c*) *The possibility of hell exists because God has given men the freedom to choose whether they will live with Him or apart from Him.*

This freedom He neither withdraws nor overrides.

APPENDIX I

THE RELATION OF THE STATEMENT OF DOCTRINE TO THE CEREMONIES KNOWN AS SACRAMENTS

The eleven Articles contain no reference to the use of baptism or of the celebration of the Lord's Supper. The Statement of Doctrine is, however, vitally concerned with the spiritual realities these practices symbolize, and with the sure and only way by which these realities can become part of personal experience.

1. The significance of the Sacraments.

Baptism by water and the celebration of the Lord's Supper are known as Sacraments. This word is commonly defined as meaning ' an outward and visible sign of an inward and spiritual grace ', that is to say, these outward acts, which belong to the material and visible world, are regarded as being accompanied by an inward experience which belongs to the spiritual world.

The Greek word translated ' baptism ' refers to the act of immersion in water. When used as a religious rite, baptism presents the idea of being cleansed from defilement. It has, however, a deeper and more searching meaning, typifying the dying and rising again as a new person. In keeping with this deeper meaning, the word is used in the Bible to signify any great transformation.

The passage through the Red Sea is called a baptism (1 Cor. 10: 2) because by it the Israelites were delivered from all threat of Egyptian bondage to begin life as a free people.

Jesus referred to His Crucifixion, His passing through death into a released glorified life, as a baptism (Luke 12: 50).

He described any experience by which His disciples shared His sacrificial pathway as being a baptism and a drinking of His cup (Mark 10: 38, 39).

The New Testament makes frequent references to baptism with the Holy Spirit (for example, Mark 1: 8; John 1: 33; Acts 1: 4, 5; 11: 15, 16) because the believer, united with Christ as his Saviour, receives by the Spirit the regenerating change this union effects (as in Rom. 6: 3, 4; Col. 2: 11, 12; 2 Cor. 5: 17; Gal. 2: 20) and becomes heir to the change this union will finally accomplish (Eph. 1: 13, 14; Phil. 3: 21; 1 John 3: 2). Paul, who spoke of ' one baptism ' (Eph. 4: 5), also taught that ' if any man have not the Spirit of Christ, he is none of His ' (Rom. 8: 9).

The meaning given to the shared bread and wine is set forth in Matt. 26: 26–28; Mark 14: 22–24 and 1 Cor. 11: 24, 25. By inviting His disciples to partake of bread and wine, Jesus was supplementing His teaching that, although His death might appear to be a terrible loss, it would be the means by which He would come to them with indwelling life-changing power.

This teaching was not confined to this occasion, nor to this form of symbolic instruction, as the following references show: John 6: 35, 51–57; 7: 37, 39; 12: 23, 24; 15: 1–6; 20: 22. John, who wrote his Gospel to present Jesus as the Source of eternal life (20: 30, 31), reported all these sayings of Jesus but omitted all mention of the bread and wine at the Last Supper.

Thus the main teaching presented by the bread and wine is of the crucified Saviour as the Source of eternal life, and the main teaching of baptism is to indicate the transformation salvation effects.

Both ceremonies are also intended to express the truth that salvation through Christ brings men into the fellowship of the Christian Church.

2. The function of the Sacraments.

(a) *These rites focus attention on three questions:*

    (i) By what means is the experience of salvation received?

    (ii) By what means is it maintained?

    (iii) What is the nature of the change it effects?

The Statement of Doctrine answers these questions thus:

(i) Salvation is received by the provision made by the coming and the redeeming sacrifice of the Lord Jesus Christ (Articles 4 and 6), by the seeker's response of repentance and faith (Article 7), and by the regenerating act of the Holy Spirit (Article 7).

(ii) The experience of salvation is maintained by continued obedient faith in Christ (Article 9).

(iii) Salvation effects the change of reconciliation, regeneration and sanctification (Articles 7, 8, 10).

(*b*) *Such outward ceremonies as baptism and the Lord's Supper can be related to the receiving of inward spiritual grace in one way only.*

Their function is to draw attention to the truths they symbolize, and to stimulate those who use them to commit themselves in penitent faith to Christ as Lord and Saviour.

(*c*) *Some have given these ceremonies a significance much higher than this.*

They regard them as being the means by which the inward work of grace is communicated, as though the act of eating bread and drinking wine when administered in a certain way, or the act of being baptized in water, have an efficacy of themselves.

This is a demonstrable error, for there is abundant evidence that many have participated in both ceremonies without receiving the inward grace they signify.

This is true not only of careless, insincere and unspiritual worshippers, but of some most earnest seekers. Martin Luther and John Wesley for years diligently sought and worked for God without a knowledge of inward salvation. During this time, as baptized members of the Church, they fully participated in sacramental observances, and as ordained men dispensed these rites to others.

It was through the word of the gospel that light came to them both. They experienced reconciliation and the inward baptism—the life-changing power of the Spirit—when they appropriated in their hearts the message that the just shall live by faith, that God waits to bless the trusting heart.

It was the gospel message that proved to be the sacramental means to their salvation. But this was the means, only in the sense that by it their minds were enlightened and their hearts were stimulated to make the response of faith. Thus the message of the gospel was the *directing and stimulating* means, and the act of God by the Son and the Spirit the *providing and imparting* means. These are the indispensable means by which salvation is received.

(*d*) *The New Testament declares that a rite is fulfilled only by those in whom its spiritual meaning is effective and active*, whether or not they outwardly observe the symbol (Rom. 2: 28, 29; Phil. 3: 3).

In the history of the Church there have been deep and continuing disputes concerning the right way in which the bread and wine should be dispensed in commemorating the Lord's Supper. There have also been disputes concerning the virtue that lies in the act. Some have held that a supernatural unction invested in a specially ordained man gives him the power to communicate the Spirit of God to others, and makes him the only channel through which such grace can come. Others have strongly opposed this idea.

It is therefore important to note that none of the company who received the bread and wine that Jesus Himself blessed and dispensed experienced any inward change. In Gethsemane they failed to watch and pray. At the betrayal they fled. From that time to the Resurrection they were without faith or hope and Peter, fresh from the influences of the Upper Room, was soon denying his Lord with oaths.

The symbolic act of Jesus was of teaching and predictive value only. The apostles did not receive His Spirit then and there.

The revealing word is found in John 7: 39, which is associated with an occasion when Jesus gave similar teaching to a much larger company (verses 37, 38):

> This spake He of the Spirit, which they that believe on Him should receive: for the Holy Ghost was not yet given; because that Jesus was not yet glorified.

It was on the day of Pentecost that the glorified Lord fulfilled the promise He had given (Acts 2: 33). He came upon them in the fulness of His risen life, so that John could later say, ' Of His fulness have all we received, and grace for grace ' (John 1:16).

This pentecostal outpouring made real in the lives of the eleven and those that were with them (Acts 1: 15) all that was symbolized by bread and wine and baptism with water. It fulfilled the meaning of all the sacramental forms the disciples had ever used—the priestly ministry of Temple and altar, the holy seasons and all the religious symbolism of Jewish life (see the Epistle to the Hebrews); so that while these disciples (not Gentile Christians, see Acts 15 and the Epistle to the Galatians) continued to observe all these Jewish forms for the rest of their lives, or up to the time of the destruction of Jerusalem, they did so in remembrance of Christ.

The transforming change was but the accompaniment and result of a greater gift, that of God Himself. The change was according to the gift (Eph. 3: 19, 20), and the cleansing was by Blood and not by water (1 John 1: 7; 1 Pet. 3: 21). There is one Priest from whom this gift can be received (Heb. 7: 24, 25), and if it is not received from Him it is not received at all.

3. New Testament practice.

(a) *The rite of baptism* was neither introduced nor administered by Jesus (John 4: 2). Forms of baptism, with water, fire and blood, were used in heathen religion.

John the Baptist used baptism with a meaning different from that associated with its use by the Christian Church. Consequently John's baptism was not regarded as being the equivalent of Christian baptism, nor as being an acceptable substitute for it (Acts 19: 1–6; 18: 24–26).

Attention was not directed to the manner in which the rite was performed, but to the significance it had for those who received and administered it.

John's baptism was a baptism to mark repentance in expectation and preparation for Him who was coming to assert and dispense the powers of the Kingdom of God. Nor was John satisfied with this symbolic response. He required that all his adherents should verify the sincerity of their avowal by 'baptizing' their conduct (Luke 3: 10–15) and by giving their adherence to Him who would come (Luke 3: 16; John 1: 29, 30; 3: 30).

The Early Church used baptism as part of the ceremony by which believers were admitted and welcomed into the fellowship of the Church. On the part of the candidate for baptism, it was an act of public confession of Christ as Lord and Saviour, and a committal to fulfil the demands of Christian discipleship. This is one of the reasons why the Latin word 'sacramentum' was adopted into the Christian vocabulary. It is a non-religious word which meant 'that by which a person is bound, or binds himself', and was the word used when speaking of the military oath of allegiance sworn by soldiers, or of the deposit by which a litigant bound himself to abide by a legal verdict.

On the part of the Church, the act of baptizing was a sign of acceptance and welcome into the Christian fellowship. No one thought the convert was being baptized in order to receive salvation. They were baptized on the ground that they were already believers (Acts 8: 36, 37; 10: 46, 47).

In the earliest days of the Church, the witness of divine acceptance and inward renewal was sometimes associated with the laying on of hands (Acts 8: 17; 19: 6), but upon the apostles and upon the first company of Gentile believers the Spirit came independently of any outward action on their part (Acts 2: 1–4; 10: 44).

Whatever difference there was in outward action at the time when the witness of divine acceptance was received, all who were so blessed stood on common ground in that they all met the divine requirement of looking to God with repentant believing hearts. As Peter declared, it is a state of heart that God honoured (Acts 15: 8, 9). This divine acceptance stands in contrast to the judgment passed on the outwardly baptized Simon of Samaria, whose heart was not right with God (Acts 8: 9–24).

The outstanding significance of the baptism spoken of in Acts 2: 38, 41 was not that the three thousand were baptized—an act which onlookers might have interpreted in a variety of ways—but that the baptism was administered and accepted ' in the name of Jesus Christ ', the One whom the national leaders had ex-communicated and sentenced to death as a cursed blasphemer. The three thousand took the dramatic step of publicly acknow-ledging Jesus as Lord and Messiah, thereby exposing themselves to whatever penalty this committal might involve (see Acts 4: 1, 2, 18; 5: 27, 28, 40 in their context). It was for this testimony, and for his claim that Jesus superseded and rendered Jewish sacramental forms obsolete, that Stephen was killed as a blas-phemer (Acts 6: 12–14; 7: 54–58).

The practice of baptism by immersion did not become universal in the world-wide Church, largely for practical reasons. There are climates, conditions and situations where this practice would be impossible. Hence many sections of the Church have replaced immersion by sprinkling, which is a symbol of a symbol.

An essential condition of salvation must be capable of being universally honoured. If a public immersion in water was neces-sary to salvation many, finding themselves in circumstances where they could not fulfil it, would be shut off from grace. On the other hand, the imperative requirement of repentance and faith can be fulfilled at any time, by any one, in any place.

(b) An outstanding feature of Early Church life was the practice of meeting for a *common meal*. This had a threefold significance. By meeting in the name of Jesus and giving Him worship and thanks in this way, believers re-affirmed their union with their Lord and testified to the impact His Lordship made on every aspect of their lives. In this way they also demonstrated the great truth that, because of their union with Him, they had been brought into a union with one another, into a bond of Christian fellowship which overcame all distinctions of race and social standing that otherwise would have kept them apart (Gal. 3: 27, 28; Eph. 2: 19; Col. 3: 10, 11). This meal also spoke to them of the heavenly feast that would be associated with the ultimate triumph of the Kingdom.

This practice came to have still greater significance and value when Gentiles came into the Church. Nowhere else in the world could Jew and Gentile, master and slave, men and women be found in such terms of equality and fellowship (Acts 10: 28; 11: 2, 3).

Thus, whereas it was important that they should meet in the name of Jesus and give Him honour, it was equally important that they should manifest His influence upon their relationship with one another. Of greater importance than the meal was the fellowship it signified. Hence the strong condemnation given in Antioch and to the church in Corinth when this purpose was betrayed (Gal. 2: 11–14; 1 Cor. 11: 17–29). These Scriptures show how possible it is to maintain a formal observance of a traditional practice while denying the purpose the custom was intended to serve and demonstrate.

Every meal is sacramental to those who partake with remembrance of Him who provides for both their material and spiritual needs, a truth specially meaningful to those who have endured the rigours of famine and prison camp life.

It is certain that the discharge of essential Christian obligations requires more than a ceremonial recognition. Such vital requirements as communion with God in prayer, the constant receiving of His grace, open confession of Christ, the proclamation of His gospel, and the need to demonstrate the unity and fellowship of His disciples, cannot be fulfilled symbolically, nor by activities that are confined to the sanctuary.

4. The Sacraments as a means of grace.

When the word ' sacramental ' is used to indicate a *means* by which men come to God and His grace comes to them, anything which is not inherently evil can be used sacramentally. Any means by which God speaks to the heart of man and induces in him some spiritual response has become sacramental to him.

The greatest sacrament man can know is the Lord Jesus Christ Himself. He is the way by which men come to the Father, and the way by which the grace of God comes to them, the indispensable way.

God has also used men to be a means of grace to their fellows. He has spoken through the prophets and apostles, and calls all His people to be a means by which blessing is brought to others.

Every Salvationist is committed to this sacramental service. It was for this purpose that the Movement was formed. The call to sanctification involves a call to sacramental living.

5. The Sacraments in relation to the Church.

All that is said above relates to the *doctrinal* foundation that directs the attitude of the Salvationist to all outward forms of religious worship. Supplementary reasons why Salvation Army practice makes no provision for the rites of baptism and celebration of the Lord's Supper are given in *The Sacraments—the Salvationist's Viewpoint* and *The Salvationist and the Sacraments*.

Non-observance of the ' sacraments ' is not regarded as being a commitment which severs The Salvation Army from other sections of the Christian Church, but as providing a contribution to Christian witness. Such a balance of practice is seen in Acts 15.

The Salvation Army testifies to itself and to others against the danger of trusting to any external rite as though it has a virtue in itself, as though spiritual grace from God can be received by an outward action that is destitute of all spiritual communion with Him, or that Christian duties of fellowship and service can be discharged by a token sign that has no supporting expression in daily living.

It also testifies against the equally serious error of allowing the non-observance of outward forms to go hand in hand with neglect of the realities they represent.

It is fully recognized that outward action can be accompanied by inward response, and can serve to stimulate it. Thus The Salvation Army does not speak against the use of sacramental forms when they serve this end.

It is good that the forms are observed, if by so doing the realities they represent are given constant prominence as vital truths that should affect the whole of Christian life. But it is also good that witness is given that these realities are experienced by those who receive and serve without the observance of sacramental rites, and thus give constant emphasis to the indispensable means by which grace is bestowed, received and expressed (1 Cor. 7: 19; Gal. 5: 6; 6: 15, 16).

APPENDIX II

THE APOSTLES' CREED

I BELIEVE in God the Father almighty, Maker of heaven and earth:

And in Jesus Christ His only Son our Lord, who was conceived by the Holy Ghost, born of the Virgin Mary, suffered under Pontius Pilate, was crucified, dead and buried; He descended into hell; the third day He rose again from the dead. He ascended into heaven, and sitteth on the right hand of God the Father almighty; from thence He shall come to judge the quick and the dead.

I believe in the Holy Ghost, the holy catholic Church, the communion of saints, the forgiveness of sins, the resurrection of the body, and the life everlasting.

APPENDIX III

THE NICENE CREED

I BELIEVE in one God the Father almighty, Maker of heaven and earth, and of all things visible and invisible:

And in one Lord Jesus Christ, the only-begotten Son of God, begotten of His Father before all worlds, God of God, Light of Light, very God of very God, begotten, not made, being of one substance with the Father, by whom all things were made:

Who for us men and for our salvation came down from heaven, and was incarnate by the Holy Ghost of the Virgin Mary, and was made man, and was crucified also for us under Pontius Pilate. He suffered and was buried, and the third day He rose again according to the Scriptures, and ascended into heaven, and sitteth on the right hand of the Father. And He shall come again with glory to judge both the quick and the dead; whose kingdom shall have no end.

And I believe in the Holy Ghost, the Lord and Giver of life, who proceedeth from the Father and the Son, who with the Father and the Son together is worshipped and glorified, who spake by the prophets.

And I believe one catholic and apostolic Church. I acknowledge one baptism for the remission of sins. And I look for the resurrection of the dead, and the life of the world to come.

SUBJECT INDEX

191

INDEX

INDEX

193

INDEX

INDEX